BIG RIG 2

MORE COMIC TALES
from a
LONG HAUL TRUCKER

DON MCTAVISH

NEWEST PRESS

LONE PINE 🌲 PUBLISHING

National Library of Canada Cataloguing in Publication Data
McTavish, Don, 1942–
Big rig 2 : more comic tales from a long haul trucker / Don McTavish.

ISBN 1-896300-71-5

1. McTavish, Don, 1942- 2. Truck driving—Humor. 3. Truck driving—Anecdotes. 4. Truck drivers—Canada–Biography. I. Title.
II. Title: Big rig two.
HD8039.M795M322 2003   388.3'24'092   C2003-910946-1

Editor for the press: Don Kerr
Interior design: Erin Creasey
Interior photos: Don McTavish. The photographer
is unknown for the picture of "Magoo and Sparky" on page 33.

NeWest Press acknowledges the support of the Canada Council for the Arts, The Alberta Foundation for the Arts, and The Edmonton Arts Council for our publishing program. We also acknowledge the financial support of the Government of Canada through the Book Publishing Industry Development Program (BPIDP) for our publishing activities.

This edition first published by NeWest Press and Lone Pine Publishing

NeWest Press
201-8540-109 Street
Edmonton, Alberta T6G 1E6
t: (780) 432-9427
f: (780) 433-3179
www.newestpress.com

Lone Pine Publishing
10145-81 Avenue
Edmonton, Alberta T6E 1W9
t: (780) 433-9333
f: (780) 433-9646
www.lonepinepublishing.com

1   2   3   4   5   07   06   05   04   03
PRINTED AND BOUND IN CANADA

Acknowledgements

Without a doubt, this book would never have been completed without the assistance and guidance of my wife, Marg Nelson. She was the one who first recognized the entertainment value of my old memories and insisted on recording them. Her expertise with written English and her blind faith in my storytelling ability have made this book a reality.

My family also deserves a huge thanks for their encouragement.

Rolf Lockwood, editor of the truckers' trade magazine *Highway Star*, really made this book possible. He was the first to read and publish my attempts at humour and continues to publish my stories, some of which appear in this book. Thanks Rolf!

—Don McTavish

TABLE OF CONTENTS

PART ONE

BAD ROAD AND
OTHER BUMMERS

UP THE CREEK

WE ALL TAKE HIGHWAYS FOR GRANTED, RIGHT? Say you order a truckload of smoked salmon from Moose Bladder Bay in British Columbia and want it delivered to your fish market in Pap Smear, PEI. No problem! There's an unbroken—and well-potholed—black ribbon all the way from Point A to Point B. Matter of fact, if you look at a Canadian road map, there are squiggly lines joining practically every hamlet and city where humans gather.

Well, I'm here to tell you, fellow Canucks, that there are scads of places trucks are expected to go where the roads don't go. Take our Arctic region and the Territories, for instance. There's a whole raft of communities and industrial sites that are frozen in all winter and surrounded by water if and when it warms up. Highways are out of the question. These hardy folks can get their mail, fresh veggies and Playboy magazines flown in, for the most part, but the heavy stuff is another story. The vast amounts of fuel, building supplies and what-have-you must move by—you guessed it!—trucks.

One of the outfits that finds highways ho-hum and prefers to rough it is Robinson Transport, based in Edmonton. Every winter, this outfit forms convoys of trucks and heads out over the ice. The custom-built plows and the mobile camp in the lead make the road as they go, with a hundred-plus trucks of all description trundling along behind, trying to keep up. Try to imagine trucking when it's pitch dark around the clock and colder than a bank manager's handshake. Literally thousands of people rely on those guys, and there isn't so much as a back alley to drive on. Personally, I never had big enough jewels to try this, but my cap is off to those brave souls who do.

Another bunch of roadless truckologists who get darned little press are the oil-patch rig movers. A road for these guys usually starts where they tear out a drilling rig at one clearing and the road ends wherever the bulldozer travels next—that is, a couple miles further into the bush.

That single lane scratched into the earth is usually so slippery that you can't stay on it. Wherever that rig gets reassembled is definitely the end of the road. I've been there, and it gives one the same feeling as writing an alimony cheque. The crude oil those guys help to find is needed worldwide, and they don't get near the appreciation they deserve, roads or no roads.

Same with the log haulers. Good grief! Some of the trails these guys have to navigate are downright criminal.

Foresters always seem to prefer the timber dangling off the side of a mountain somewhere. I kid you not—dropping down the side of a mountain, fully loaded on a trail built for two weeks' use, can be a real bum squeezer. Some of those landings in nosebleed country feel like you've driven off the planet.

Call me a wuss, but I couldn't wait to truck on something with lines painted on it, something that didn't end when I got where I was going. Believe me, those log truckers sure earn their money.

When I finally got the chance to do some hi-miling, I foolishly figured that I'd seen the last of that end-of-the-road stuff. I got a job with a haul-it-all flatdeck carrier in Edmonton and ran my company-issue, cabover Kenworth all over western Canada. Most of the miles were pretty routine, I must admit, with the usual weird snags thrown in that all drivers have to contend with. I did quickly discover, however, that this outfit also had a few end-of-the-road destinations. Rats!

Turns out one of their main customers manufactured all sorts of steel stuff for mines scattered through western Canada and beyond. We hauled to most of them, and wouldn't you know, the majority were right on top of mountains! Climbing to the end of some of these mine roads made for some really memorable moments. You know— memorable, like your hemorrhoid operation, for instance. Actually, I whine for no good reason because the steel bars, balls and bolts we hauled to those sites were "jammy" freight.

Without a doubt, though, one of these trips to a mine was the granddaddy of all my where's-the-bloody-road stories.

As soon as I got my running orders at our Edmonton terminal for this particular mine load, I smelled something rotten in Denmark. For one thing, those rusty old oil drums full of steel balls were loaded on a sawed-off thirty-six-foot-long trailer that we used mostly to get into tight spots. Second, this load was going to a new mine north of Vancouver, toward Whistler, which boasts some really high mountains. The third ominous sign was the written instruction to stop at our Vancouver terminal for final directions. Major "oops!"

Soon as I arrived there, the situation took a king-sized dive when I was told to move two drums from the back pile to the front, over my drive axles. Yahoo! That was four thousand pounds that I was obviously going to need for climbing traction wherever I was going. The last bit of bad news, after I was handed a map, was to stop at a certain shop in Squamish and pick up a two-way radio tuned to a pre-set channel. Jeez! Now I couldn't wait to get there and see what a kettle of dead smelt I'd been talked into.

I turned off the highway a few miles short of Whistler at a piddly little sign with the mine's name on it. It turns out that logging trucks are running on part of this trail and have the same radio channel as I do, so with their help I proceed from wide spot to wide spot, until I'm past all the chatter. I'm climbing steady and although it's May or June, there's snow in the trees along the trail. After almost two hours of creeping along and silently thanking the genius who suggested overloading the drivers, I pull up at the end of the road.

No mine, no sign, no nothin'. I assured myself it was the right road, but all I could see was a wide, shallow creek flowing into a ditch alongside the road. All of a sudden, a voice comes over the radio.

"Just stay put! I'll be there in a few minutes," says the voice.

Well, I'll be darned! I didn't think God needed to use a radio, but I was sure He was the only one who could see me up there. Minutes later, the biggest grader I'd ever seen—it was a 16 F or G or something Caterpillar—came thundering down that creek! It had immense tire chains all the way around and an inflated truck tire mounted on the front as a pusher.

He roars around behind me, butts up against the trailer, then radios me again.

"The mine is two miles up the creek," the voice says. "Steer around the bigger rocks and straddle the water. Just take it slow and enjoy the ride."

Yeah, right! We're going straight up, bouncing over rocks the size of basketballs with water flowing over them and I'm supposed to relax!

That big, old grader was so heavy and powerful my meager cabover hardly had to work at all, and minutes later, we break over the top, where sits the missing mine. A picker truck and a few miners are ready to unload me as soon as I grind to a halt and I'm empty in a jiffy.

I questioned the grader operator's road-building skills, pointing at the creek. This gained a snicker.

"Why bother?" he says. "This works, and we didn't have

to disturb that little creek. Besides, the miners I push up here every day in the bus get a great kick out of it. The mine's only going to be here a year or two, so no use getting fancy!"

I suppose he had a point, but the only ones who got to see that creek were a handful of miners, truckers, and a few mountain goats who ventured that high up. Needless to say, I came down like an eagle in a power dive, and still thank my lucky cowboy boots I only had to haul one load up the creek.

COVER THE TOMATOES

L ET'S SAY SOMEONE MENTIONS THE MONTH OF January in Canada. What's the first thought that comes to you? No, no, not the Visa bill with all your Christmas expenses on it. Cold weather, right? In fact, depending on which part of the old Moose-and-Maple-Leaf you live in, extreme cold comes to mind.

I spent a large chunk of my life in northern BC and Alberta, where even the thermometer threatened to freeze solid on occasion. I must admit, those prolonged super-cold stretches don't seem to occur much these last few years. (I wonder if I'm so old I caught the end of the Ice Age? Nah!)

Anyway, there were weeks-long periods of cold that hovered around the minus-thirty-five mark. Stone me if I'm wrong, but that's about where Celsius and Fahrenheit meet, I think. That number was real important, because any colder than that made even steel brittle and the Compensation

Board, as well as the school boards, would suggest you stay home. I promise not to hang up on the bleeding obvious, but every man, woman, and bed-wetter who chose to live in this national refrigerator could dress for—and learn to cope with—the cold.

It was a whole different can of sardines for machinery. The family four-wheeler would usually fire up if the engine block heater was plugged in and the battery didn't let you down, but those diesel-guzzling eighteen-wheelers were another story. Believe me, most folks have no idea how complicated it is to keep the rigs running through the winter. Granted, there have been some super improvements over the years, but they only happened because of the problems we had.

Start with the fuel. Smelly, old diesel will freeze. Oil companies that supply the stuff add jet fuel (kerosene) to it soon as winter sets in, and by mid-winter, we're up to 50 per cent mix. This stuff won't freeze, so end of problem.

Next hassle was—and still is—air. Compressors blow hot air into miles of big and little air lines connecting a mountain of tanks, valves, and "brakey" stuff. This causes condensation, which can freeze up anywhere along the line and plug the system, same as Aunt Emma's perogies did to your arteries. Nowadays, we pump the air through a dryer, but we didn't have that contraption then. We poured enough alcohol through our lines to keep the whole rig wasted for months!

Matter of fact, we were expected to climb under the tractor and trailer at trip's end and open these tappy-type things called drain cocks, and the fumes alone could give you a cheap high. Man, I'll tell ya, sliding under the rig at thirty-five or forty really separated the men from the hairdressers. For me, climbing under was certainly preferable to starting down a long hill somewhere, pressing on the brake pedal and nothing happens. Boy, does that ever give you a weird reading on your heart monitor!

Next problem was expansion and contraction (pretty scientific for an old mileage-stacker, eh?). Just a few seconds use of the air brakes makes the shoes and drums hot. As long as we're moving and tapping on those brakes once in awhile, all's well, but look out when we park! The metal brake drums shrink as they cool, pressing the shoe so tight, they freeze together. When you see a trucker pounding hell out of trailer wheels with a steel bar, he's not penting frustration, he's trying to shake the brakes loose.

You ever notice trailers that run north have lines painted on the sidewalls? That's so we can see in our mirrors if the wheels are turning. One "dual" can be frozen, and we can't tell we're dragging it until we see the smoke from a couple of burned up tires.

Would you believe that grease freezes when those double-digit minus figures occur? Grease turns to glue, especially on fifth wheels. A great cure for constipation is moaning into a curve, turning the wheel, and Old Fang keeps going in a straight line across the road. Ya-bloody-hoo!

So remember—motor oil, guys. Throw away the grease.

So far, we've been yapping about rigs that are still mobile, but shut one off for a few hours in extreme cold, and you've got your steel statue. I had tons of experience with trucks stiffer than a pointer's nose staring at a dead duck. The Edmonton-based outfit I was sentenced to only had shop space for half the fleet. We always made sure there was room for our bulldozer and one heavy bed truck inside, so they could pull-start the tin popsicles.

Just tie on and tug, eh? No way, Nellie!

You might get the engine to turn over that way, but the oil in the pan would be like week-old gravy, and the block would commit suicide before the oil would start to flow. It was Ol' Donny on his belly under the truck, with a propane tank and a big heater nozzle called a tiger torch. Trick was to get the oil pan heated up without setting the old girl on fire.

When I think of all the winters lying on my stomach at minus-thirty degrees, plus a stiff Prairie breeze, it's a wonder I was able to father a couple of kids. Anyway, when the pan was warm, and a little heat on the rear ends allowed the driver axles to turn, a liberal squirt of ether and a quick yank from the winch truck usually did the trick. Those cold 250 Cummins engines would hammer like a rivet gun and belch smoke, but before you could finish an Export A, she was purring like a kitten.

Oh, jeez, before we wander off cold-starts, I've gotta tell you about old Ernie. He was our bookkeeper-slash-comptroller, cranky as hell and somewhere between sixty and ninety years old. Bullheaded as they came. His pride and joy was a 1960-something, four-door Cadillac. No matter how cold it got, he would park in his usual place, five feet from a plug-in for his block heater, but he would never bother to plug it in. He claimed this clunker would start in any conditions, using his own method. Every two or three hours, he would run out, squirt a batch of ether directly into the carb and turn the key. By God, a couple of cranks and she'd fire up, with a small bang and a cloud of smoke.

Well, one day, when you even had to bring your brass monkey inside, Ernie again ignores the plug-in. He goes out three hours later, blasts away with the ether, turns the key and gets nothing but a low groan. He says nothing, but goes back inside and returns two hours later. More ether. He turns the key, and there's a lower moan than ever. End of the day, he's back out with his can of ether and really gives her a hefty squirt.

By now, everyone, including Ernie and the shop foreman, are aware the old hearse is going to need a boost, so out come the batteries and cables. Good grief! Old Ernie gives 'er yet another squirt and already anybody within ten feet of that car is getting sleepy. He turns the key, and there's a massive explosion! The lid on the air cleaner careens off the open hood about the same time the oil pan hits the ground.

Ernie steps quietly out of the car with his eyes the size of dinner plates. He locks the car door as if it was still possible to steal the thing with the motor in pieces, and he goes inside to calmly call home and get the kids to pick him up. We never talked about this episode around Ernie, and he never brought it up.

The only guy who ever mentioned it was goofy Robbie, who would stick his head in Ernie's office every once in awhile, holler "boom!" and then run like hell.

We've covered the machinery problem pretty well, but what about the poor, old driver? I drove a cabover Kenworth, which, I dare say, is one of the coldest rides you can get. For those of you unfamiliar with road cruisers, the ones with the long noses are called "conventionals." The driver sits behind the nice, warm engine and behind the steering wheels that are throwing snow up into fenders. No problem staying warm in those babies.

Now I'll give you an idea what a cabover is like. Turn two chairs sideways, one on either side of your kitchen table. The table is roughly the size and height of a Kenworth "dog-house," really the roof of a tunnel running from front to back, right through the middle of the truck. The engine is inside that tunnel, so we sit on both sides of it. Any heat off that baby goes right out the back end.

Now put a cookie sheet up against your knees. Picture you're sitting six feet in the air, right overtop the steering axle with the snow shooting up right under your feet. Now, my friends, you've got your cabover. From the waist up, she's a shirt-sleever, but down around your cookie sheet, she's colder than a fresh grave.

Mind you, macho dudes like we were didn't complain. We covered our knees with our parkas and stopped every once in awhile to stomp circulation back into our feet. Heck, we hardly even snivelled about the cold. When it got down around minus-thirty, one of us would mention that we hoped the wife thought to cover the tomatoes.

STUFF IT *WHERE*?

"**W**AIT A SEC!" I SAID. YOU WANT ME TO BACK this fifty-three-foot trailer up in there? I'm sorry sir, but you must have me mixed up with Harry-freaking-Houdini! It'd take a magician to stuff this trailer into that mail slot!"

Sound familiar, gang? I'm absolutely sure that all my fellow wagon-draggers have run into situations like these. As a matter of fact, I'll bet my big, brass belt buckle—engraved with "I Bring Joy to Women"—against your collection of Willie Nelson cassettes that it's happened more than once to every trucker. Jeez, it seemed to happen to me regular.

I don't suppose I'm a truck-rodeo-class backer upper, but I could usually plop the trailer where she was supposed to go. Heck, most freight docks with rubber bumpers and bright lines painted on the road make it so easy that your Aunt Millie could poke the back end up to a door. With a little patience and a lot of swearing, we can usually wiggle these rubber-mounted box cars into some pretty tight spots, but every once in awhile, look out! On some occasions, the shipper or receiver walks out to the street to meet you and takes you for a half-mile walk through an obstacle course. Then he points into a corner.

"Drop her there," he says, nonchalantly.

When you mention that he'll have to take down some fence and remove a corner of his building, you'd get the usual line.

"Lots of guys have backed in there."

This called for the standard reply.

"Not with a box this long, they didn't!"

"Oh, do they come in different lengths?"

Duh. You can bet your first born they do.

As far as drop-off bays went, there was a handful of real doozies we had to face on a regular diet that were barely doable. One of my nightmares was a manufacturing plant in Port Moody, just outside Vancouver. This thing was built at the tip of an ocean inlet, almost at sea level, with high mountains on two sides. The fog would roll in off the ocean and engulf the whole area for days. We're talking pea soup here, and looking down from a cabover, you couldn't see the road. You kind of crawled around the back of the plant where the shipping door was, guided by yellow flashing lights mounted here and there. Pull your T-shirt over your head while you're driving and you'll get the idea.

There was a bright yellow line painted on the road, leading from the shipper's bay out into the lot. You'd pull alongside this line as straight as possible, so you could see it (on occasion) out the driver side window. A couple of plant workers would walk alongside, hollering directions as the trailer approached the invisible doorway. On top of the fog, another problem was the fact that the doorway was a tight squeeze. The inside of the building was blacker than a coal miner's hanky, and the guys doing the guiding assumed that you had radar. It was a lot like trying to get a wet noodle into a wounded cougar. Somehow we always made it, but what an experience that was.

Another plant that took first prize in the "stupid ramp" category was one that I hauled to in Richmond, another suburb of Vancouver. To start with, these guys hadn't bothered to put in a dock at all, which meant "hand truck" or "hand flog" from the back doors. Needless to say, we were all pleased as a pigeon in a park full of statues when the company agreed to a ramp.

Boys, they created a nightmare. They bashed a hole five feet deep, fifty feet long and nine feet wide into the warehouse floor. They figured the trailer deck at floor height all the way around would be great for loading flat-decks. Good point, I suppose, but a trailer is eight feet, six inches wide. That left three inches of clearance on either side, which wasn't a whole hell of a lot with rain running down your mirrors. We always managed it, although we must have looked like we were watching a ping pong match, glancing from one mirror to the other.

That same plant expanded, and this time they installed a real beauty. They dug a tapered trench about one hundred feet long, ending at trailer height at a door. Easy to get at, and lots of room, but it had one small problem. This building was at sea level, and they forgot about the water table. Every time the tide came in, that trench would get three feet of water in it! Of course, the unholy amount of rain that fell in this part of the world would collect in there too. Lots of drivers flat-ass refused to back in there, not knowing how deep it was or how solid the bottom was. Can't say as I blame them.

Another knee-slapper I had to contend with was in a residential area in Surrey. I was dispatched with an empty, forty-five-foot, hi-cube box to load for Hay River, NWT. One quick look at a map showed me that I was heading into a crescent of some sort in an upscale neighbourhood. I arrived at a well-kept house surrounded by a manicured lawn and a piddly, little, gravel driveway leading along one side of the house. A long-haired professor type walks down to the truck from the house, and points to the driveway.

"Back it in there," he says.

"Believe me, sir, you really don't want me to do that. I'll slaughter your lawn and that gravel path. Maybe you're wiser to load here on the street."

"That's not an option," he tells me. "Come with me and I'll show you why."

We follow the gravel driveway past the house and up to a two-car garage with a bit of an extension on one end. He opens the door, and that garage is stacked wall-to-wall and ceiling high with triangle-shaped pieces of plywood, along with some odd-length lumber.

"This all has to go in your trailer, Sonny. It'd take us a week if we carried it all to the street."

Brother! He had a point there.

"What the hell is this that you're shipping all the way to the Territories, anyway?" I asked.

Now Donny not lie! Turns out it's a large, wooden igloo that the Canadian government paid this guy to design and build. It was some kind of meeting hall for the Inuit.

Being a taxpayer, I suddenly no longer cared a rat's kazoo about protecting the professor's property, and I cut him a couple of drainage ditches right up to that garage. I left him the empty trailer and I can just imagine how much deeper those ruts got when the loaded trailer left.

Sheesh! What next?

I end this literary masterpiece with a problem I had getting a trailer out of a warehouse rather than with backing one in. Actually, backing the low-slung, step-deck trailer into this outfit's door wasn't all that tough. Not a lot of room to spare, but a couple of wiggles, and in she went.

A few minutes later, an overhead crane comes overtop, carrying a rectangle-shaped metal building which it sets down on the trailer. This thing resembles an airport control tower with glass windows all the way around, and I'm told it's a control cabin for a lumber mill. Well, I start strapping it down, but the gable roof on this gizmo looks awful wide, hanging over either side. A quick pace of the doorway tells me we're in trouble. I point this out to a foreman, who looks at me like I wandered away from my nurse.

"No way it's too wide!" he claims, but out comes his

tape measure and two minutes later, he's muttering to himself and turning the colour of a tail light. He goes to a nearby phone and flaps his arms so much while he's talking that it looks like he's trying to fly.

Anyway, minutes later, four men show up and—would you believe?—they dismantled a strip of the building's metal wall and part of the door frame. An hour later, I slipped out what was left of the doorway and never looked back. For once the ballup wasn't my fault, but I'll bet the engineer who designed that thing had to get major plastic surgery on his old keester after he got it chewed out by the brass.

Gang, they don't give truckers near enough credit. When you come right down to it, we're all doorway-ologists!

MAJOR "OOPS!"

RELAX, GANG! EVERYBODY MAKES MISTAKES, AND I'm sure the ones you made weren't worth a roll of Canadian quarters compared to the beauties I've witnessed. Like Old Man Murphy once mumbled, "If something can go wrong, it will." Someone else claimed, "If it's got zippers or tires, you're gonna have trouble with it."

Believe me, folks from every walk of life—from the garden-variety skinner like myself on up to the guys who own a whole mountain of fancy iron—pull off real bloopers from time to time.

The goofiest mistake I ever heard involved a brand-new cabover Freightliner. This beauty was one of eight that the Edmonton-based outfit I was with had just taken delivery of. We're talking state-of-the-art, with lots of chrome, 425 Cummins power, and every do-dad but a blender. Two of them get issued to the Calgary branch, and three weeks after they get there, one goes missing. The driver had parked it by one of the shop doors early in the AM and left the keys in it so that the bolt-twisters could service it first thing. By mid-morning, someone finally connects the dots and realizes it's been pinched. The cops and insurance people get involved, but with little to go on the case goes colder than a penguin's keester.

A couple months later, a rather shady-looking dude shows up at our Edmonton terminal truck shop in an obviously old and abused pickup truck. He locates Krusey, the shop foreman, offers a used thirteen-speed transmission for sale (cheap) and leads him out to show it. There's no moss growing on old Krusey, and one peek at that gear box tells him that there's something rotten in Poughkeepsie. There's not a mark on the tranny, and although someone had taken a stab at messing up the serial number, some of them were still readable and resembled seven others we owned.

Krusey says, "You got a deal! Hang in right here, and I'll call over to the office to cut a cheque."

Office, nothing! He dialed 911 and got the law on the way, pronto. The guy must have had the brains of a sack of axe handles because he hung around until he saw the cops coming, and he was way too late to run. A quick reference to the numbers, a couple of days' investigation, and a farmer in southern Alberta was arrested with a whole barnful of truck parts, including what was left of our missing rig.

Turns out the old sodbuster was subsidizing his grain quota by stealing trucks, stripping the parts for sale, then burying the cabs in his farmland. Heck, he hadn't even had time to bury ours! Someone said it was no wonder he couldn't grow anything. He had so many cabs buried, the farm was solid steel. Talk about a major mistake! If that greaser had taken that tranny to any other shop to resell it after buying it from that chop-shop, those two low-lifes would probably still be in business.

There's a couple of driver-mistake stories that just kill me when I think of them, and here's the first one.

A newly-hired driver had only made one trip for us from Edmonton to Vancouver and had returned. It was branch-to-branch both ways and went without a hitch. His second trip was to take him to the Cominco smelter in Trail. Late the following afternoon, the Vancouver dispatcher gets a phone call from this new driver. He asks how to get to the Cominco plant.

"You see the tall smoke stacks?" asks the dispatcher.

"No stacks," says the driver.

The dispatcher asks what side of town he's on, and the driver replies "the east side."

"That's funny!" says the dispatcher. "You should be able to see those stacks. What can you see?"

"The Port Mann scale, where I'm phoning from."

"Oh, Jim Dandy. You're just outside Vancouver. You're supposed to be in Trail, two hundred miles back. Look at your bills!"

There's a few seconds' silence, then a very sheepish reply.

"Oops! Heh, heh. I'll call you in the morning."

Click!

Boy, it's no wonder dispatchers get ornery.

The other episode involves an owner-operator who didn't stay with us long. He arrives in Vancouver late and is given his return load orders over the phone when he calls the dispatcher's home. He was to bobtail to a plant in a small town east of Vancouver and pick up a "spotted" (stationary) trailer. It happened to be one those shippers with a half-dozen loading bays and trailers from different carriers filling them. At this particular time, three belonged to us, and the other three were owned by other companies.

The dispatcher instructs the guy to just hook to the loaded hi-cube van and pull it to Edmonton. He couldn't supply a trailer number because the shipper had gone home, along with everyone else, and had only guaranteed a trailer would be finished.

"I'll handle the paperwork tomorrow," says dispatch.

Well, tomorrow opened up with a bang! The first call was from the shipper who was hot enough to light his cigar by just blowing through it.

"Why didn't that bleeping load roll last night? What kind of bleeping, blooping service are you running there?"

Click . . . buzzzzz!

The second call is from the enemy.

"Is it possible that one of your retards took the wrong trailer? I've got a tractor sitting at the plant with no trailer to yank."

Good grief! Our trailers and theirs are fleet equipment, covered in four-foot letters, with company names all over them. Couldn't happen, you say? Well, it did. We got the professor stopped at the Kamloops scale, and after confirming that he had the other outfit's trailer, he offered an explanation.

"You told me to take a loaded trailer and this one was in the best shape."

As it turns out, both loads were headed for the same city, so a fast agreement to pull each other's trailers solved the mixup. It's a toss-up who made the biggest mistake, the operator who shopped for the wagon, or the guy who hired him.

Wouldn't you know I'd save the best blooper for last? Don't you love it when the boss makes the big mistake? I'm aware of the unwritten law that states (a) bosses never make mistakes, and (b) if the boss makes a mistake, refer to rule (a).

Well, here is what the Grand Poobah—the owner, no less of the company I slaved for stepped in. He personally had contracted to truck a D8 bulldozer from Edmonton to Saskatoon, promised speed-of-light service, and then discovered that we had no tractors to spare. He couldn't beg, borrow or steal help from anyone. We had one of our city-licensed rigs load it, so it was sitting on a company lowbed, all ready to go. The boss happens to be standing in the dispatch office when a fairly new, pretty strong-looking tractor bobtails into the yard. The old man growls at Wally, the dispatch, to hire the guy if he's looking for work, tie him onto that dozer and kick him out of town.

"That'll blow holes in your background check and test drive policy," says Wally.

"We'll do it when he gets back," says the boss.

Wally makes it happen, and the Marquis de la Diesel is on the phone to his client soon as the tail lights disappear.

"She'll be there in the morning!" he declares.

By noon the next day, two phone calls colour the day grey. Number one is from the customer, howling "where in the bleeping-deleted" is his machine?? Call number two is from the Queen's Finest, asking if we had seen a stolen truck, the description matching exactly with our newly-hired owner-op. Need I tell you that our trailer and that freaking dozer disappeared like a lead life preserver? We almost felt sorry for the boss. NOT!

His luck held, anyway, as three weeks later, one of our guys spotted the empty lowbed hooked to an old beater, and he called the cops. That laid paths to (a) a farmer near Battleford who had bought the dozer, (b) the stolen tractor parked on the crook's acreage, and (c) our newest owner-op, who got major time in the slammer.

There! I'll bet a set of chrome wheel nuts you're feeling better.

SHORT STUFF

I FIGURED MY WAY OUT OF A PICKLE THE OTHER day. I had a whole raft of funny experiences that I wanted to pass along to my fellow members of the Gear and Steer Society, but none of it was long enough for a single story. It finally dawned on me that I could make a bouquet of this stuff. It's sort of all over the map, but then again, so are we truckers. Right?

This first shortie finds good old Nicky and me in a Quesnel, BC, restaurant having supper. The place was on our flight plan to Vancouver. While we were eating, a young man and woman came in and sat down in the booth behind me. I couldn't help but overhear their conversation, which sounded like the guy was insisting on going to a motel. I overheard the woman say no, she wouldn't go, but the guy kept pressing, and his voice was loud.

Now I'm no prude, but I was getting a mite tired of the

hollering, so as I slid out of the booth, I quietly asked Nicky to back me up if this got nasty. I was always real brave with Nick around because he was built like a fire hydrant, with no neck and big arms. His black Italian eyes made him look real sinister.

I took a couple of steps back and stared at the anxious lover.

"Knock it off, guy! She says she doesn't want to go with ya."

From the guy I got a wide-eyed stare. But would you believe, the girl jumps out of the booth and looks me right in the eye.

"Mind your own goddamn business!" she says. Then she turns to the guy. "Come on. Let's get out of here."

She and Larry Lovelorn stomp out, hand in hand.

I sheepishly slide back into our booth and see Nick grinning.

"I was ready to jump in, but that girl didn't look so tough," he says. "Anyway, you're still my hero!"

It took two weeks for the kidding to subside over that.

Another quickie involves Million Mile Max and a newly-hired spare board youngster. We were all convinced this new guy had been a little careless with the truth on his application because he was nervous as a canary in a roomful of cats. We figured he hadn't done any winter driving in the mountains although he claimed different.

The story goes that Max is climbing up the east side of Rogers Pass with Nervous Norman in the jump seat. It's uphill for miles on the way to the summit, and the farther up they go, the worse the road and weather get.

There had been no need for jewellery on the drivers until about three-quarters of the way up. Then that cabover Kenworth with its forty-foot load of steel bars wipes her feet on an icy section. By now it's snowing so hard, you can hear the flakes hitting the ground, and Max's attempt to chew down to pavement to hold the rig on the hill long enough to throw on chains is as useless as diapers on a buffalo.

The rig starts sliding backwards. Max releases the brakes and lets her roll, sending his paranoid partner ballistic. When the rig is rolling back fast and apparently out of control, Max gently steers the trailer into the snow-banked mountain face and hits the brakes. The trailer bangs into the snow bank, grabs on and whips the whole rig across the road. Then the front of it heads down the hill. Max is already in gear, and at what seems the perfect time, he starts chewing. Out pops the trailer from the snow bank and they're headed back downhill at a controlled rate. Well, that was the last straw for God's Gift to Trucking. He sat there with eyes the size of headlights on a Hudson.

God's Gift got off at the next stop and took the bus home. Last I heard, he was driving a three-ton around town for Eaton's. According to him, Max lost it and should have been put away. As Max has it, steering the rig backwards for ten miles wasn't an option, so the only thing he could do was turn around and drive back to a flat spot to chain up. I think I'll go with Max's story although I doubt I'd have the fixtures to pull it off myself.

This next knee-slapper involves a real "pro" skinner

nicknamed Yabadaba. Ah yes, yet another Ukrainian with a "sounds like" name.

Anyway, he departs Edmonton in the middle of a prairie winter storm, heading for Vancouver via Calgary. By the time he arrives in Calgary, hours late, she's a full-blown monster storm, with drifting snow like mad. He decides to wait it out and gets a hotel room near the Trans Canada Highway.

It's colder than a complaint department clerk, so he leaves his trusty KW at fast idle through the night. At sunup, he wanders out, and there she is, gone. He looks around a bit, determines the snow isn't deep enough to bury a cabover and realizes it's been pinched.

Unbeknownst to poor old Yabadaba, his rig had already been found. One of the other company trucks heading east on the Trans Canada came across it, pulled over to the roadside heading west, about seventy miles out of Calgary. The eastbound driver discovered the rig shut down with nobody around, so he walked into a nearby ranger station.

Oh yeah, they know about it. Someone had also stolen their four-wheel drive ambulance overnight and was last seen heading west with it. A phone call from the ranger station to the guy who owned the trucks set the situation ablaze. The owner was one of those guys who could break a beer glass just by staring at it. By the time poor old Yabadaba called in to report the theft, the Old Man was already hotter than a tamale.

"My truck's been stolen," Yaba says, "and when they catch the creep, I hope they string him up!"

The boss screamed so loud through the phone that Yaba claims he still has a hearing problem from it, years later.

"I know where my blankety-blank truck is! It's where you should be, instead of playing blankety-blank tourist in a blankety-blank hotel! Catch a blanking ride to the ranger station west of Banff, clean the snow out of the blink-blank breather and get that blankety-blank load to Vancouver, you (blankety-blank, deleted)! If they find the crook, I'm going to hire him and fire you! Now get your (deleted) in gear!"

Click.

Believe it or not, Yab and the Old Man were pretty close, and it was only when you messed with one of his beloved trucks that the spit hit the fan.

This last donation still makes me laugh when I think of it. It's another one of those "drive the owner into a frenzy" stories. I take you way back to when I'm just getting started as a diesel demon.

Things are kind of slow one day, and the boss elects four of us to do a little "freebie" for him. Seems there's an old skid-mounted wooden shack near the steel mill we were contracted to. This shack had to be moved. Apparently it had been abandoned by the mill so the boss had been using it for years to store old tires, rims, parts and what-have-you. Now the steel company wanted it back for one of their other plants about five miles away, so we were elected to move it.

The plan was to drag the tires and stuff out of the shack, drag the whole thing onto the oilfield trailer we had, and use a winch-equipped truck to pull it. The other three guys were old-timers and hated doing something for nothing. We're halfway finished unloading the junk when one of these guys discovers a gallon jug of clear liquid.

Now, these guys were all born-and-bred farmers, and it took mere seconds to determine the liquid was moonshine. Hell, they even identified the brand! A sniff and a finger-lick convinces Zorro that it's Walter Hominiuk's, while Chips is sure that Steve Chernawyncan ("SHERNA-winshan") produced it. The jug gets passed around, and my little snort won't even stay down. I didn't get sick or anything, but my body just rejected that jet fuel. A half hour later, the first sign of these guys getting stewed occurred.

"Let's just drag the shack over to where we're going," one of them says. "The roads are icy, and it'll save some time."

"Hic!"

Far be it from freckle-faced me to argue, so they drop the trailer and tie the winch line to the shack. Then, with two guys and the jug in the winch truck, and me driving the half-ton behind, and the drunkest of the three sitting beside me, away we go.

That shack slid along those icy side roads easy as you please, and those two nuts flew along like the thing had wheels. We finally arrived at the paved highway that we had to travel on for a mile or so, and I appeared to be the only guy who saw that it was bone dry. They hurled onto the highway, damn near swinging the shack into the far ditch and just kept flying, with pieces of the skids peeling like a banana.

Now, I'm not sure whether something flammable

tipped over or the wooden skids got hot enough to ignite, but the shack was blazing when we turned off the highway. The guy with me was passed out cold, and the other two got a few steps from the winch truck and fell over.

I obviously had to call the boss, and was I scared? Do rubber boots make your feet smell? He was so hot, he was speechless for once. He banged the phone down and showed up at the crime scene minutes later. He just shook his head, told me to take the truck, go get the trailer and park it at the yard. No way I'll tell you the heat those three guys got into. It's too horrible.

And you thought truckers had no fun!

PART TWO

COOL DUDES

ROAD ROYALTY

I KNOW DARN WELL THAT MOST HI-MILERS GET AS big a kick out of our "King of the Road" image as I do. I discovered at a very tender age that most people were as curious about long haul as I was. In my case, there was no question that trucking was what I'd end up doing.

I must admit, though, at fifteen or sixteen years of age, I first figured that gynecology would be an absolute hoot. And I only dropped the idea once I found out I couldn't pick and choose my patients. From then on, I pursued trucking with a vengeance and finally graduated to highway work and hi-miling.

I was amazed by how curious people were when I admitted to grinding gears for a living. I've been to parties with college types who lead fascinating lives but prefer to hear about icy hills, heavy loads and whiling away the hours behind a wheel. Maybe they figured I wouldn't understand

Shakespeare or care what temperature plutonium melted at. Nevertheless, I got a charge out of all the attention. Of course, I never told them our trade secret.

Most of us drive for a living to get away from people.

I don't think we're anti-social, but we sure as hell are loners. Now, don't strain your pacemaker. I didn't say we weren't friendly! Matter of fact, some of my happiest moments were sitting around a cafe, beer hall or drivers' room, swapping stories with the other mileage merchants. I think we truckers just prefer to talk in short spurts. Jeez! I remember team driving with some guys where conversation never rose above a grunt or a nod for days on end.

True happiness for us all is barrelling down the road at whatever speed the truck or the law will allow, the gauges all in the green and over two hours passing by since we ate at Shirley's Eat-It-and-Beat-It with no sign of being sick yet.

I suppose our occupation is murder on family life, but we usually come home happy. I imagine dealing with the public every day could make you a little miffed. I'm a bit shy, like I suspect many of us are. So we can't really take any credit for the "King of the Road" title. Most of us just do the time, keep our noses and our drivers' licences clean, with no hero thoughts at all. Hollywood made us look good and the newspapers make us look bad, but I think our real image exists thanks to a handful of our guys who "done good" when they were called upon or who were just plain colourful. I met tons of these types in my day, a few of whom I'll blow by you to make my point.

Fast Eddie was one of the hero types. Actually, we had

to give him this short nickname because his last name was unpronounceable. It was Ukrainian, and sounded something like "guts and cabbage." Anyway, Eddie is parked in a pull-off up in northwestern Alberta late one night, trying to catch a little shut-eye near a railway siding. He happens to notice smoke coming out of one of the end box cars in a long string of same along the track. Moments later, flames start shooting out around the door.

At this point, most of us would have sharpened a stick and got out the weenies, but not F.E. He dollies off his trailer and bobtails onto the tracks at a nearby crossroads. Then he chains up to a couple of boxcars—including the burning one—opens the coupler and drags the cars away from the rest of the string!

Minutes later, one of the local railroad dudes shows up and glad-hands old Eddie like crazy. Eddie ended up with a few bucks' reward and a letter of commendation from the railroad. Better yet, the story ended up in the Edmonton newspaper, and we all came out looking like kings.

Would I have done what Eddie did? No pea-pickin' way!

Another colourful character who added to our royal image was Sinful Sid.

He was an unofficial driver-trainer for the fleet I worked for, and he got all the "greenies," including me, for our first few trips through the mountains. I swear, those cabover Kenworths we drove ran so much better when Sinful was in them.

No root or snort, no bang and crash, no tailgating or

stupid moves around the tourists. Lucky for us, this king of the road passed these good habits on to a thousand guys like me, bless his diesel-pumping heart.

Ah, but old Sid did have one failing—foul language. Matter of fact, that's how he got the "Sinful" moniker. He could not string two words together without throwing in something crude. Even when he just climbed out of the bunk, the conversation would curl your hair.

"Well, f——n' god damn! If we ain't arrived at the mother-f——n' gag and f——n' puke already! I'm f——n' starvin'! Let's get the f—k in there and get some of that sh—t they call f——n' vittles!"

I usually ordered something I could eat with my fingers, because I hate to admit how many places asked us to split. Even the company branches usually gave Sid a pin-to-pin switch to keep him away from the customers. The other drivers and I didn't notice it all that much after awhile. We all used the same words, but we weren't as generous with them as old Sinful.

Eventually, Sid bought a big-mother bed truck and went to work up in the Arctic or Territories somewhere. Good thing, because the only ones he could piss off up there would be the polar bears.

There's no doubt in my feeble mind that we inherited our lofty "King of Road" title from the old pioneer truckers, back when you could open the windshield with a little crank on the dashboard. I'm referring here to the drivers of the 1940s and 1950s, when trucks started really competing with the nasty railroad.

There were already lots of trucks around by then, but the missing ingredient was good road. I can proudly state that as soon as the government started building freeways and laying asphalt, our boys were out there pounding it to pieces! Granted, 185 horses or so couldn't travel the speed of sound or anything, and those old engines smoked like poker players at a high stakes all-nighter, but they trucked across Canada nevertheless.

Nowadays we think twice about leaving the terminal if the retarder is acting up, but with these guys, even brakes were optional.

I was lucky enough to work for one of those gutsy trail veterans, and he was definitely a true Road King. Old Simon was a loaded pistol with thinning hair, the temperament of a wounded grizzly, and enough trucking experience to fill an encyclopedia.

He starts out in the 1940s in construction, helping build the Alaska Highway. Then, in the early 1950s, he buys a used Autocar tractor and goes trucking across the country for Trans Canada Freightlines. In 1954, he partners up with a couple of equally-experienced truckers and forms a six-rig outfit that grew into a huge, present-day fleet. There was nothing the "old man" wouldn't transport, and those fearless drivers he hired would nurse those old trucks of his into the worst places Canada had to offer.

One of the drawbacks to trucking for an old pioneer like Simon was that he wasn't real impressed with modern technology. If he did it with 185 horses, why the hell did you need 250?

"Spring loaded seats?" he'd holler. "Just don't hit the holes so hard!"

"Engine brakes? Forget it! Slow down on the hills."

"Upholstery in the cabs? Next you'll want curtains in the windows!"

I must admit that those old hands and I never complained too much. All the trucks he owned, from his cabover Kenworth, long-haul fleet to his winch-equipped bed trucks and scads of every semi-trailer imaginable were all strong and dependable. Eventually, he mellowed and ordered all the latest do-dads in all his new equipment. He'd never admit it, but he was as proud of those chrome-covered, big-power rigs as we were.

One of the highlights of my life was sitting in on a bull session with Simon and his crew of hi-milers, talking about the past. Finally getting invited to join in—for a kid like me—was like getting a college diploma. After hearing stories about where these old timers had trucked and how they got there, I was convinced they were the start of our royal strain.

Gang, idle down your six hundred horses a little, set your cruise control, drop the pressure in your air chair a smidge, turn down the stereo, and belt out a cheer for those old pioneers!

TOUGH LIKE KITTENS

'VE SAID IT BEFORE, AND I'LL SAY IT AGAIN. TRUCK drivers don't get near enough recognition. They don't get much positive press at all. How often do you come across an article like "Local trucker makes uneventful three thousand-mile trip" or "Mystery trucker helps family in distress"? Like, never.

Only the bad news goes public. Well, I've got a whole raft of stuff here that shows truckers have hearts as big as their rigs. Go get the Kleenex because this is a real tearjerker.

My first example involves a big, burly, hi-miler lease operator named Snoopy. He loads a big used industrial road packer one day, somewhere in Oregon, destined for a construction company in Alberta. He heads up to the Canadian border, crossing at Blaine, Washington, on his way to our Vancouver terminal for fuel and paperwork.

Now, we all know that the Yankees and Canadians

alike frown on trading dirt, plants, and stuff like that over the border, so these machines, new or used, have to be steam cleaned until they're spotless. This one looked clean enough to Snoop, but the Canada Customs folks insisted on an inspection anyway.

They poked around under the hood of this brute, and be damned if they didn't discover a bird's nest tucked up in an almost invisible corner. The nest came complete with a mother bird and three or four chicks. Cold, hard fact was that the nest and its contents would have to be removed and destroyed before that machine would be allowed to enter Canada.

"Those little ones look almost old enough to fly," says Snoop. "I can't mess with this."

The big, tough Customs agent agrees and figures the chicks will be strong enough in a week or two, so Snoop gets on the phone to the Vancouver dispatcher, who's equally moved. He, in turn, calls the construction company to explain.

Well, would you believe that all these guys involved decided to dolly the lowbed off at the border and wait until those chicks flew the coop before the nest and the machine were removed?

Tough guys, huh? Pussycats!

Anyway, six or seven days later, the company sends a tractor at no extra cost to pick up the lowbed and machine when Customs finally called to report that the nest was empty. It had been removed and placed in a tree nearby. The contractor had rented another machine to fill in until they got their own back.

Cute, eh?

Another Good Samaritan project that has been happening every Christmas for years—and may still be going on to this day for all I know—goes like this. We were approached at our Vancouver terminal years ago by a group of nuns driving a beat-up, old station wagon. They had a whole slew of cardboard boxes full of donations that they had collected for the poor. They wanted these boxes shipped to Edmonton, where nuns of the same order would pick them up at our terminal and distribute them.

They had no money, and with those long, black uniforms, I doubt they even had pockets. The big rub here was that the boxes contained perishables: glass, baking, and all sorts of stuff. We couldn't just throw them into the end of a dry box, or they'd freeze harder than a ballpeen hammer. It all had to be carried in the cab, which literally filled the sleeper, with a few items spilling onto the jump seat. This meant (a) that the truck taking them would have to run single, and (b) that the poor schmuck who got them would have to sleep on the doghouse.

Ah, jeez! With those four nuns and those pleading eyes, who could refuse?

One of the guys headed that way and running single volunteered—he must have been Catholic—and the show was on. Those four nuns fired boxes up to the driver as fast as he could stow them in the sleeper. Then they gathered in front of the cab and blessed the whole rig. Then they gathered around the driver and blessed him into next Tuesday.

You should have seen the grin on that gear masher's

kisser when he pulled out. He figured he was on a mission for God. I don't want to get spooky on you, but this guy had great luck for the next year. No flats, no nothing. Every year after that, when the nuns showed up in Vancouver, all the drivers fought to see who would get the boxes and the blessings. Figured it was a free ride to heaven, I guess.

This next offering shows that a whole trucking company can have a heart. Years ago, a local school board approached the manager of our Vancouver terminal with a proposal regarding their Interesting Occupations Program. Junior high school pupils were asked what appealed to them as a career, and the school board would try to arrange tours of the various choices.

Well, driving big rigs was way up the list for both boys and girls, so we agreed to some day trips. This, of course, is an insurance company's nightmare, but somehow the Grand Poobah got the okay.

I was pulling trailers around town at this point, and every morning for two weeks, I'd have some wide-eyed kid waiting at the terminal, just itching to spend the day in that conventional Kenworth. Before I even started the truck, I'd let them pull the horn chain, push and pull all the buttons they wanted and then let them sit behind the wheel for a few minutes. I'd answer as many questions as I could—good grief, there were thousands—and then, with all that out of their little systems, I'd warn them that if they touched anything while the engine was running, I'd break every bone in their puny bodies.

That worked like a charm, as I never had to slap even

one little sweaty mitt. I'd buy them lunch at whatever truckers' stop we were near and always introduced them to the other drivers as my partner. The other skinners always played it serious, and you should have seen some of those little duffers beam. I know for a fact that most of those kids will remember their days as long as they live, and I still remember all that as if it were last week. Now is that a civic-minded outfit, or what?

While we're in the "good old company" mode, there's another short heart-warmer I'd like to unload. A French Canadian guy shows up at the Edmonton dispatcher's window one morning and applies for a job. He's just arrived in Alberta with a wife and two kids and is pretty desperate for work. He's in his forties and has a bit of a hunched back, besides being a stranger to the Prairies.

So he's not a perfect candidate.

He's told that there are no openings, but he gets permission to hang around the drivers' room when he asks. He's carrying a lunch bucket and a new pair of gloves, which indicates he's pretty serious. Every day at 8:00 AM for the next week or so, he shows up in his old car, waves to the dispatcher and plants himself in the drivers' room. Finally the owner comes by one day and approaches the dispatcher.

"Who's that guy hanging around the drivers' room?" he asks.

He gets the full story, walks out to talk to the guy for a few minutes. Then he orders the dispatcher to let the guy fill out an application, take a look at his driver's license and get Vern to test-drive him.

"Anybody who hangs in like that deserves a shot," says the owner.

Now, this is not the owner we know and love. The one we know hates everybody, including his relatives. He assumes all truck drivers are lazy and that they steal from him. Giving someone a break doesn't fit his profile. Turns out, though, that Frenchie's an ace trucker, strong as an ox, even with the bad back. He stays on with us for years.

Goes to show you, a little compassion can go a long way in this business.

That's enough about the other guys and the company. What am I, chopped zucchini? I too have mellowed for my fellow man. Take the trip Sparky and I are in the middle of, one hot summer day in the BC Cariboo country. We're running with an empty flatdeck all the way to Vancouver out of Endako up north because that wonderful mine we unloaded at had no ore to haul to the coast. We may have been frying in that cabover KW—who ever heard of air conditioning in a company truck?—but we were rolling flat out and making lots of wind.

About ten miles out of Clinton, we come across an old car with its hood up and a huge travel bag tied to the roof. Dad and a couple of six-to-eight-year-old kids are waving like crazy. We pull over, hike back to the car and discover a pretty worried family. It's getting dark, they've been there for hours with no one willing to stop, and the family clunker has quit. The smell of burned oil spells trouble, so we offer a lift into Clinton.

No way! They can't leave the car for fear of theft, and

the family insists on staying together, come hell or high water. There's no hope of finding a mechanic to come out there at night, so guess what? The old boy has forty feet of sturdy rope with him, and the only thing we can do, other than abandon them, is to tow old Jezebel and family to town.

We convince them it's best for Sparky to drive their car because we can read each other's minds if something goes wrong, so we stuff the whole family into our oven of a cab and drag that dead hunk at twenty MPH into a town garage.

God, you'd think we'd handed them a million bucks! Kisses from the missus, hugs from the kids and broken bones in our hands from old dad shaking them so hard. We parted company feeling pretty pleased with ourselves, but being macho dudes we couldn't show it.

"Well, there goes our lightning schedule," says Sparky.

"Yeah. Bloody tourists," says I.

Sorta moves ya, don't it?

GEARJAMMER GENIUS

I'VE ALWAYS THOUGHT OF MY FELLOW POTHOLE professors and myself as born problem solvers. As people who really think on their feet, or on their keister, in our case. Whether we haul cars, cattle, canned goods, chemicals or swingin' meat, we all have one thing in common—the rig.

It's only a machine with lights and chrome all over it, so it can develop a glitch in a split second. How many times have we been trucking for hours over highways flatter than Swedish pancakes and cobwebs forming on the gearshift, when something goes haywire? You immediately go from brain-numbing boredom to adrenalin rush to prevent whacking into a cliff or trying to stay ahead of your wagon, which just got a mind of its own.

With our rigs as big, heavy and fast as they are, any of the above could have catastrophe written all over it. Joe Average has no idea how many necks have been saved because a quick-thinking trucker did the right thing—or the impossible. I witnessed this problem-solving ability right from the start, with the diamond-hard dudes who trained me to gear and steer.

Just months after being hired by an Alberta flatdeck carrier, I was dispatched on the first of many weird assignments and one of the most memorable. Two gas-driven, single-axle V-liners, with tandem thirty-six-foot decks, and one winch-equipped gas burner with a track-mounted front-end loader headed for an abandoned mine site in the foothills of western Alberta. I went along as a helper.

The Luscar Coal Mine had shut down years ago and the town buildings and mining equipment had been auctioned off. We were on our way to load up some of the stuff that our boss had bid on.

We chained up all the trucks at the mine turnoff, as the last ten miles up the mountain stretched over an overgrown goat trail that hadn't seen a truck this size in years. We were supposed to unload the dozer at this point and follow him in, but the ideas started to fly and one of the old vets told us to walk the dozer right up to the front of the float.

"All that weight will give the winch truck lots of traction," he said.

Simple nods from the others and away we went, with the dozer dangling on the nose of the trailer and the four driver tires bulging out like Grandma's girdle. It was the middle of winter, and the cold made the ice cleats on our tire chains stick to the road like gum to your Tony Lamas. With that overloaded winch truck in the lead, plowing drifts and chewing ruts for the others, it was almost like a Sunday drive with the missus.

With about an hour of daylight left, we broke into a valley and there sat the abandoned town, covered in snow and missing only smoke from the chimneys and the miners themselves. We looked over the first couple of houses we came to, noting that they still had blankets on the beds and dishes in the cupboards. I tell you, it was creepier than a truckload of tombstones.

However, we had bigger fish to fry. It was already colder than a bob-sledder's behind, and the temperature was dropping. We were going to be up there for days, dismantling and loading what we'd come for, so food, fuel, and sleeping bags had been brought along, Our biggest worry was keeping the trucks and the dozer mobile.

At thirty-below, the gas engines in our trucks could be idled up and kept running until the cows came home, but that Allis Chalmers crawler with its Detroit diesel engine got real cranky in the cold. It had block heaters, but the nearest electricity was ten miles away, which meant a major extension cord. On the other hand, leaving the crawler run for days was out of the question. In no time at all, it would carbon itself up and die of heartburn, not to mention that the hydraulic oil would turn to oatmeal.

The two wisest of our rag-tag team pointed to a huge mansion hanging over the town a short distance away, which was our next stop. We walked through the huge front doors into a living room of sorts, with a stone fireplace covering one wall. Without a word, one guy found a way to the basement, and another started pacing the width of the doors. Two more nods and grins, and then just minutes to get a fire going in that fireplace. The wood for it was still stacked nearby and there was a whole bin of coal downstairs.

Houston, we had a plan!

It seemed a crying shame to walk a bulldozer over that gorgeous hardwood floor, but hey! The front doors opened wide enough to clear the old girl, and the timbers under the floor would support a half-dozen of these babies. The joint was due for demolition anyway, so I figured the mine owners who built this palace wouldn't care. Half an hour later, the old girl clanked and roared up the front steps and through the doorway, nosing up to the blaze. That old pebble-pusher never had it so good! She purred like a kitten the four days we were up there. We crashed near the fire every night ourselves, turning what could have been a really gerstunken job into a high-class camping trip!

Sheer genius, I tell you. The chances of my thinking of stuffing that dozer into that mansion would be on a par with playing poker with the Pope.

Talking about thinking quick and making the right moves reminds me of a situation that'll bring some of the Rogers Pass vets to tears. We all had to face Field Hill near the British Columbia–Alberta border. It was a miles-long grade with varying degrees of slope, and I swear that sucker had its own cloud. It seemed to snow ten months of the year up there. Half the problem came from a major LTL carrier called Gill Transport, which ran a zillion single-axle A-trains, pulled by single-axle cabovers.

Well, that was just tiddly when the road was dry, but look out when the snow fell. Even triple-rail chains on that one axle didn't guarantee climbing to the summit, and with those guys running convoys of five or six rigs at a time, Field Hill was regularly dotted with spun-out Gill rigs, all zig-zagged across the road, sitting in the ditch or dollied off rear trailers. This meant that the tractor would have to come back down for them.

The tandem drive tractors most everyone else ran, including me, had hardly any trouble at all, once we were chained up, but we had to manoeuver around Gill's units. This got pretty heart-pounding, with rigs sliding down one direction and rigs scratching up the hill in the other direction.

Pandemonium! But take a bow, boys. There were lots of near-misses, but not one kaboom that I ever heard about. In true tradition, we renamed the place "Gill Hill" and even though tandem tractors quickly replaced those singles, the name stuck for years. How embarrassing for Gill, huh?

Okay, back to business.

My last example of "Wow! How'd you think of that?" reared up awhile back in BC's Fraser Canyon. A couple of need-to-knows are (a) anyone who lives in a cold climate is aware that frost coming out of the ground in the spring plays havoc with the highways, putting waves in them like a windy lake, and (b) semi-trailers, like tankers and vans, are set and rigid like a lawyer's rates, but flatdecks are flexible and bend in the middle like mad. Sparky (the Wise) and me (the Green) are pounding old Unit 16 westbound through the Canyon one spring morning with a flatdeck load of very bendy reinforcing steel. We're travelling as flat out as that old 250 will allow when we drop into a shallow dip and then into a frost wave. Sparky and I go airborne and the same time we come back down into our seats, there's a hell of a cracking sound.

Sparky pulls over right quick, and we wander back to eyeball a gaping four-inch crack in the ditch-side outer steel rail of the flatdeck. We aren't going much farther like that, as one more small bounce will snap the other side and it'll be belly-to-the-road time. The usual problems crop up: we're miles from help, still 150 miles from Vancouver, where we're headed, with not enough cash between us to hire a welder. The word "credit" always sent shop guys into hysterics. Sparky started swearing and pacing, which was good, because he could think better when he did that.

Bingo! A few minutes later, he points to a pile of railroad ties lying by some track nearby. We help ourselves to a few of these, stacking them under the frame near the crack. Then we dolly off the trailer and that split closes up tight. A couple of ties laid along the top of the rails alongside the load of steel and straddling the crack were chained tightly into place. Then we backed under the trailer again.

Up she came, straight as you please. We figured that this patch job would just get us up the road a bit, but stone the crows! She held all the way to the coast.

I lie to you not! This sort of problem-solving goes on all the time among our Levi-covered legion. If you aren't convinced that truckers are smart, just ask them about the square root of "pi." They'll tell you right away that it can't be done, that pi are round; cake are square!

The final proof of our high IQ is our payroll. We all calculate in our heads how much we've earned, and our numbers are always higher than the bookkeepers, right gang?

BIG STAN

I'VE GOT A CONFESSION TO MAKE, GANG. WHENEVER I was asked what my most memorable trip was, I would ream off a few that stuck in my mind about piloting the rig. Truth of the matter is, my most unforgettable and hair-raising run happened when I was fifteen years old, hanging with one of the truck-driving gods I had the good fortune to have had befriend me.

Big Stan T—I'd write his full name, but I can't spell it—was one of those six-foot-plus, Levi-covered, quiet types, built like a grizzly bear and just as snarly. You know, the kind of guy you avoid eye contact with, just in case it sets him off. I kind of doubt Big Stan would have turned and run if you'd beat on a pot and made lots of noise, though.

Like most big guys, Stan turned out to be a pretty mellow dude when you got to know him, and he was sure good to old Donny. I'm sorry to report that Big Stan cashed in a few years ago, and I really miss the big ape. He and I were buds for over twenty years, and he died way too young. This story is dedicated to him, and I promise you'll get as big a hoot out of it as he would have.

On second thought, I just had a vision of Stan, towering over me saying, "Donny, Donny! Why you want to write about me? Dat not what pipples want." Old Stan sure slaughtered the Queen's English. Anyway, back to the story.

Like I mentioned, I was only fifteen, back in the mid-fifties, pumping gas at an all-night service station (remember those days when gas was five cents for a truckload, and attendants actually dashed out to gas you up and put greasy fingerprints on your hood while they pretended to check your oil?). At this point, I could only dream of driving truck and would have crawled over a pile of used oil filters just to stand where one had been parked.

Enter Big Stan and his tandem axle, gas-driven, 427 International body job tanker. Stan had cut a deal with the service station owner that I worked for to park his rig on the property, which was only a block from his home. Midwest Tankers, the owners of the truck, had their own yard, but it was out of the way, so this arrangement suited Stan. Like all us gearslappers, most trips started in the middle of the night, and it was no different for him.

Well, needless to say, I took to that truck and Big Stan like a Swede takes to pickled herring. I was on a late shift one night, and when things got quiet, I climbed up on the running board of that big, beautiful tanker, to get a look inside.

Good gravy! Big Stan comes around the front and catches me standing on the truck.

I had said "hi" a few times to him in the weeks past, so I was sure he recognized me, but he had only nodded and I had been told that truckers eat their young, so I froze.

Hold the phone! Big Stan was smiling. I just might live through this.

He reaches in his pocket, pulls out some keys and says, "Hey, kid! You want closer look? I unlock door for you."

"You bet, sir!" or some other sucky thing was all I could say.

He let me sit behind the wheel and explained what the buttons and levers were for, while I pictured myself in heaven with the gassy, oily, sweaty smells and the feel of the big steering wheel in my clammy hands. When Stan offered to take me on a trip one day, I darn near passed out from happiness.

A couple weeks later, Stan pulled into the station just as I started a 3:00 PM-to-midnight shift. He mentioned that he was loaded for Jasper Park, and if I wanted to go along, he was leaving around 1:00 AM. I would have postponed a liver transplant to go along, so I agreed on the spot. I snuck away mid-shift to eat and was all set to go at the appointed time.

I tell ya, I felt like a king sitting in that jump seat with the roar and the smells all around me and Stan slipping through the gears and manoeuvering that big tanker like it was part of him. Back then, that trip west from Edmonton to Jasper Park was on two-lane roads, connecting small town after small town, climbing and dropping through the foothills, which was absolutely fascinating for the kid here.

Actually, the road was paved all the way, and with spring around the corner, only the ditches and fields still had snow.

Six or seven hours into the trip, Stan asks if I'm sleepy, having worked a full shift before we left. I immediately shout back, "Hell, no! I've never felt so wide awake. This is great!"

"Oh, yeah? Maybe you don't think it so great when we got to climb. Not be scare. I've been to same place lots times!"

Turns out we weren't headed for the beautiful, relatively flat town of Jasper, but up to Miette Hot Springs (so shoot me if I've spelled it wrong) off the main highway and up the mountain about ten miles.

We pull off the highway into a clearing at the bottom of the hill. Stan jumps out and puts tire chains on all four driver duals. From what I can see, there are bare patches on that trail, and I'm thinking a full set of tire chains is a bit of an overkill, but my mom didn't raise an idiot, so I kept my trap shut. Less than halfway up that winding, narrow, steep grade, conditions changed, big time. This trail had obviously been plowed a few times, but there was darn near a foot of fresh snow on it up here, and I could hardly tell which way the road went.

Big Stan didn't look all that worried, but he wasn't saying much, and little as I knew about trucks, we were obviously in a very low gear. The engine sounded like it was working pretty hard, and I could feel the truck lurch as the chained-up wheels spun every once in awhile. With me on the edge of the cliff side, able to look down on occasion and seeing snow-covered rocks, tree tops and the road where we had been, hundreds of feet down, the situation was a tad unsettling.

Just about the time I started to regret going along on this suicide mission and thinking maybe I should look into something safer, like lion taming, we arrived at the summit, with the hot springs buildings and maintenance camp looking like civilization again.

Stan pulls up alongside a huge storage tank, bails out and hooks up his transfer hoses as if he had just tip-toed through the pansies. I walked around, looking in buildings and acting cool, but inside I was a trembling bucket of mush.

An hour or so later, we're headed back down that toboggan run, still chained up but going a whole lot quicker. With the chains draped back on their hooks and us flying east on our way back to Edmonton empty, it occurred to me that Stan must have known I was nervous as a turkey near Thanksgiving when we climbed that mountain, but he never said "boo."

I think it was on that return trip that I switched from thinking that I could never handle that kind of thing to thinking, "By cracky, if Stan can do it, maybe I can!" I still figured gynecology would be a fun way to make a living, but thanks to Big Stan, I went looking for icy hills to chew up instead.

A couple years later, I found a flatdeck carrier in Edmonton that took a chance on me. By the time I was able to earn my chain-drive wallet and Levi jacket, Midwest Tankers had sold out to their competition and Stan had ended up with us. It was fabulous working with him, and I tell you true—you too, Stan, if you can hear me—he always treated me as an equal. And even though I could follow in his footsteps, I could never fill his shoes.

As time wore on, I got talked into taking a dispatcher's job, but passing orders to Big Stan never felt right. Nevertheless, he always followed them and never moaned any louder than the rest of us.

Stanley, you were a class act. The only time I ever had bad thoughts about you was when I was lying in the snow under my truck, hooking up tire chains. At those times I wished I'd hung around doctors rather than diesel demons.

PAVEMENT PILOTS

LEMME GUESS. YOU'VE JUST BEEN SERVED A COLD burger and day-old fries by a truck stop waitress who's ignored you for half an hour. Things were a little testy at home when you left on this run, and the shipper took all day to load your wagon, then snarled that the load was rush and it bloody well better be on time. You're firmly convinced that at least sixty of the 425 horses under the hood have fallen asleep because the old girl just ain't pulling like she should. You're feeling insignificant and thinking maybe you should've gone to work in the bakery with your brother.

Well, cheer up amigo, and just chew on this idea for a bit. The most comparable industry to trucking is the airline business, and in our racket, you, sir, are the pilot! You could even wear one of those sharp, short-sleeved shirts with the shingles on the shoulders. I'm sure you already have those macho aviator sunglasses. The only thing you should hold onto are your western cow-pie kickers. We'd look silly in shiny Oxfords, right?

The only difference between us and the airlines is that we don't get airborne, although we sure try like hell on a downhill straight stretch. They may have their runway, but we have the highway. Just picture a chrome-soaked hi-miling tractor with a matching paint job on the trailer and a gob of marker lights glinting in the sun. It's as pretty and as power-ful a sight as anything Boeing ever spit out. Your cockpit has almost as many switches, gauges, and warning devices as those flying tin tubes. They have all that radio stuff, but we don't get lost as much, I guess, so the CB is plenty. Their equipment looks bigger than our rigs, but pull the wings off theirs and what have you got?

How about the payload? We can stuff fifty thousand pounds onto a thirty thousand-pound truck and a whole lot more if nobody is looking. Let's see the airline stick on more than the plane weighs. You want to talk Jumbo Jet? Check out our Super B-Trains and our accessory-equipped lowbeds. Truth is, whatever cargo they fly to a destination goes onto one of our trucks for final delivery. So there!

I suppose their major commodity is a little different, considering they fly people around, if the flight isn't can-celled, that is. Well, we could haul people too if we wanted to, but who needs the aggravation?

You want noise like an airplane? I'll give you noise like an airplane. An engine brake crackling through straight pipes downhill and through a tunnel comes darn close.

Heck, even our turbos scream like jet engines except on a little smaller scale.

Speed, hustle, rush! Everything's a big-mother panic, so shippers tend to use planes a lot. Big deal! Some truck or other has to pick up the freight at the shipper's door and haul it to the airport. It sits in a warehouse until it can get crammed into a neat, little container that'll fit on the tin crow. Eventually, the sucker is airborne but ground crews at the destination have to reverse the procedure and stick the load back onto one of our trucks for delivery. If the stuff doesn't have to fly over water, it's darn near as fast to leave it on the first truck and laugh off a few extra hours. Matter of fact, whoever picks up the tab probably saves scads of cash, too.

Speaking of ground crews, we go through an almost identical procedure as the airlines do. While the mechanics are crawling all over the rig, replacing worn parts, smearing grease on the seats and wiping the glass with oily rags, the drivers are in the pilot's room getting their flight plans and weather reports. The only difference is that we *go*—rain or snow. Whoever heard of de-icing an eighteen-wheeler before she taxies out?

We had a great bunch of knuckle skinners at our shop and I was always amazed at how much they could get that diesel thingy to run or that doo-ma-hickey that makes electric work. I had a shop foreman years ago put in a sixteen-hour shift to complete the motor job on my rig as well as other stuff that cropped up. He dropped the cab over the engine, told me to climb aboard and fire it up. Ten seconds after the engine started, it began to snow in the shop!

The foreman chopped a finger across his throat and just hung his head. He'd forgotten to remove a rag he'd stuffed into the turbo to protect it while he worked on the engine. Those shredded bits of rag had gotten into everything on their way to the chimney. He was faced with another bunch of hours to dismantle all the exhaust thingies and clean out the confetti.

Did he throw his wrench through the windshield, like I would've done? Nope. He just said, "Your flight's been delayed. See you noon tomorrow."

Back to the ground crew. Our freight-handling procedure is almost the spitting image of the silver buzzard guys. They pull up to a gate; we back up to a door. In a plane, half the freight walks on. In our cattle liners, all the freight walks on. In a plane, the side doors to the freight hatch are opened, and a crew with lifters cuts loose. In our hi-cube freight hatch, the rear doors are swung open, and a crew with conveyors or forklifts attacks the load.

You see? Same-same.

Anyway, once you're reloaded, you're captain of the whole shooting match again.

Now you're faced with the same problems as the winged freighter. You have to keep a sharp eye on the gauges, the way ahead and, in our case, the mirrors, which Ace doesn't have to contend with. If either one of you does something stupid, it could turn into a catastrophe. The only thing we got going for us is that if our engine quits, we're already on our runway.

Actually, hauling people is no big deal either. I carried a

load with a conventional Kenworth and a forty-eight-foot dry box awhile back. I was on my way empty to a pipe company to load fittings that were going who-knows-where. The pipe company was located in the lowlands of Burnaby, just outside Vancouver. I turned off the main drag and started down the grade of the side road within blocks of where I was going.

I stopped when I came upon a whole army of people wandering on the road ahead of me. That two-lane road had turned into a lake, with the deep ditches on both sides full of water, and a foot or better covering the road for blocks. I recognized a couple of mugs in the crowd as belonging to the warehouse guys who had to load me, so I offered a ride. The other thirty or so folks who also worked on the far end of this road-turned-river started bugging me about riding in the trailer.

Well, the trailer had just been swept out, and it was drier than a month-old muffin, so what the hey? Two women who didn't like the idea of hiking up their kilts to get into the trailer jumped into the cab and the rest clambered into the back. I tied the barn doors open and, to hear the laughing and yapping in that van, you'd think I was hauling them to Disneyland.

I waded through water up to two feet deep in spots, just crawling to keep the wave down and making sure I stayed where I thought the middle of the road should be. As we got closer to the dyke holding back the Fraser River (which was the cause of this mini-disaster), the water level dropped until we were back on dry land, where these three or four companies were situated.

I was as big a hero to those people that morning as any pilot might have been who'd landed a troubled plane. I bet they couldn't wait to get home and tell their kids they got trucked!

Turns out the humongous pumps that transfer water out of those two canyon-class ditches over the dyke to the river couldn't keep up with the Vancouver shower we'd had the night before. Mind you, if you looked straight up during one of those things, you'd drown!

I have no idea how that gang got back to their cars at day's end, but it was no never-mind to me. They'd only purchased one-way tickets and they were "standby" at that!

Well, my fellow double-clutchers, I bet you're feeling a whole lot better now. Leave the fries, skip the tip, and walk proudly out of that burger joint.

You are cleared for departure, Captain!

PART THREE

MECHANICAL
MIGRAINES

WHAT'S THAT FUNNY NOISE?

EVERY OCCUPATION HAS ITS TRYING MOMENTS, and trucking sure has its share. For the most part, gear grinding is an absolute hoot, and most of us drive because we love it. It sure as hell ain't done for the money. You meet darn few filthy rich truck drivers.

There are some things truckers dread, and without giving away some of our trade secrets, I'll tell you about a few that my fellow wagon draggers and I have experienced. Some are just piddly, like being served funny-smelling meat at a strange truck stop or waiting days for travel orders in a city a thousand miles from home. It's the stuff Joe Average will never have to experience that I want to lay on you.

How about getting behind a four-wheeler the size of a lawnmower, with Mom, Dad, and a handful of bed-wetters hurling down a two-lane road at twenty miles an hour, pulling a holiday trailer twice the size of the family beater? You can count on the road having more bends than a box full of pretzels, and the oncoming traffic looking like a state funeral. You've got to hang back a ways because you never know when little Suzie might feel sick and Dad will anchor his little import and its mobile motel in the middle of the road with the car nosed onto the shoulder.

I darn near clobbered one of these July gypsies in the Fraser Canyon once. I'm hanging back, waiting for a third lane wide spot that I know is coming up pretty quick, and I can see a couple of young kids in the rear trailer window waving and making faces at me. I wave back, thinking that it's pretty dumb for those kids to be riding in that trailer. All of a sudden, the kids spin around, and a woman who obviously devours a whole pot roast at one sitting appears in the window. But all that weight shifting in the trailer is more than Dad can compensate for, and he swerves all over the road. I've got to hand it to this guy, because he gets that twister back in a straight line and pulls over in the first wide spot he gets to. I'm hugging myself for leaving the extra road between us as I come within feet of piling into him. What do you wanna bet that guy filled his Fruit of the Looms?

Another trucker's dread is the stupid truck breaking down. Does it happen in a city, next door to a repair shop? Not likely, Larry. Usually it happens in the middle of nowhere, or in a town with a population of ninety, including the dogs. You might get a hay rake serviced there, but that's about it. You can get to a phone, though, and that's where the fun starts.

What with cell phones, CB radios and such, the problem may not be quite so severe any more, but one fact remains: the driver is the captain of this asphalt battleship and really has no idea what happens in the engine room. You flip a switch or push a pedal and you're off like a bride's pyjamas. Who the hell knows or questions why?

Okay, so here we are, broken down in Sour Cream, Saskatchewan, and a tow truck that can haul forty tons is non-existent. Now we have to explain over the phone to a mechanic what's happened to our trusty steed, so that he can arrange a repair.

I guess we all have a rough idea what makes 'er tick. Personally, I know that if you lift the hood, there's this big chunk of steel with six holes drilled into it and some belty things bolted on. I know if you pour some diesel into one of the holes, blow some air in and put the lid on, the bottom of the hole comes up, squeezes the fuel until it blows up, and that pushes the bottom back down. If you do this repeatedly to each of these holes, you've got your diesel engine.

Somehow, all this violence gets transferred into a big steel box full of wheels with teeth on them. God only knows what happens in there, but now the power flows down a long pipe called a driveshaft. Then it goes into two pot-bellied things near the rear wheels. Fast as you can say "pass the tabasco," the power is at the wheels and you're rolling.

A few years ago, this mechanical marvel was pretty simple, and a well-placed hammer tap or piece of tape could get you on your way. Not any more. It's a plumber's nightmare now.

Okay. So you're on the phone to the shop foreman, and this weird conversation starts.

"What broke?"

"Well, the engine just quit."

"Any lights come on the dash?"

"Yeah. Three on the top row and two on the bottom row."

"Anything dripping out underneath?"

"No."

"How does it smell?"

"Smells normal."

"Any noise before she quit?"

"Yeah. Kinda like tacka, tacka, tacka, wheeeeeze."

"You hear anything like grinda, grinda, thok?"

"No."

"Ah, well then. We're laughing. It's probably your torque bligger. There's a thing on the side of the block that looks like a small Coleman stove. Look for a little wheel underneath and turn it tight, counter-clockwise. Then start her up and head to the dealer in Regina."

Sure as hell, he's right! How do they do that? It's like a doctor doing a hemorrhoid operation over the fax machine.

I think surprises are next on the dread list. The best example of this that I can think of happened to my fellow pothole seeker, Fast Eddie. I wish you could meet this guy. My life would have been a bore without him around. Anyway, he's on his way back to Edmonton from somewhere in Saskatchewan, running his empty single-axle V-liner and forty-foot tandem flatdeck. He stops to pick up a hitchhiker dressed in an army uniform near Lloydminster late at night in the middle of the winter.

The stranger claims he drives truck for the army, and because Eddie's as pooped as a bartender at a bikers' convention, he decides to let the soldier drive. Story goes that the guy is a little rusty but stays between the ditches, so old Eddie drops off. Awhile later, Eddie wakes up to a tap on his shoulder. The driver points out the windshield at something.

"What do you think those flashing white lights are?" he asks.

Eddie takes one look, then reaches over to grab the steering wheel fast and reefs them into a snow-filled ditch—ending up parallel to, and just a few feet away from, a freight train flying by. Eddie realized that the flashing white lights had been car headlights blinking between box cars at an unmarked rail crossing. Talk about lucky! Hell, other than having to put tire chains on to back out of the ditch, he wasn't even stuck. Surprises like that we can do without.

The biggest dread of all, at least, certainly mine, is getting stranded. In my day, most drivers always carried a tool box, a few spare parts, and some canned food because you just never knew when the rig might develop a serious glitch or the weather or something man-made might leave you on your own. Wind storms in the Prairies blow lots of snow, leveling fields-with-ditches-with-roads into one flat surface. One trip, my team partner and I had to take turns walking in front of the truck, poking the snow with a bar to find the road edge until we could get into a small town on a back-road short cut we decided to take (like idiots).

My worst experience almost cost me my miserable life. I'm driving one of about fifty trucks moving a dismantled oil drilling rig about eighty miles off the nearest highway, near the Territories border in northern Alberta. Usually these moves are short and there are trucks ahead and behind all the way, but we were moving this thing hundreds of miles and the trucks got all scattered out. The turnoff from the highway onto the bush road was well-marked, but then it got tricky. It was colder than a bill collector's third notice, and the wind was blowing across that frozen muskeg, covering the truck tracks ahead of me.

As any oil patcher will tell you, the area near a drill field is crisscrossed with bulldozed trails that the seismic guys create, and sure as taxes, I went down the wrong trail. At about the same time, I arrived at a dead end with no way to turn the rig around. The gas engine in my old IHC hic-cupped twice and quit.

I have no idea how cold it was, but I knew it had frozen the gas line, so pick a temperature. My sleeping bag was stuffed into the headache rack outside—smart, eh?—so it was of no use to me. The load of steel pipe I had on wouldn't burn worth a darn, so I figured a nap across the seats was in order. Like all twenty-something-year-olds, I felt immortal, and dying never entered my mind. Lucky for me, the truck push (foreman) was counting trucks and went looking for me. I woke up in a warm pickup cab with little or no feeling in my hands, feet or ears.

Well, with a little massaging and a whole lot of pain, everything started working again. My blood circulation caught hell, mind you, and my hands still ache when I open the fridge.

To this day, if it ain't on the map, I don't go.

MINE'S BIGGER
THAN YOURS

ONE OF MY NEIGHBOURS DROPS BY THE other day, looking a little on the sour side. Old Orville should have been in a good mood because he'd just got back from a driving holiday up in northern BC with his Missus, but such was not the case. I figured he must have found bugs in his roses or some other earth-shattering problem, but it turns out he was mad at me and all truckers in general.

"Why do flippin' highway trucks have to be so big?" he growls out.

Well, like any red-blooded Canadian, I blamed it on the government, claiming they wanted us to carry more freight to reduce the number of trucks on our roads. Pretty quick thinking, huh?

Unfortunately, we still weren't off the hook. My usually-mild-and-calm neighbour throws his arms in the air and hollers some more.

"One of your damn big trucks almost killed me and Mildred!"

I didn't have a clue how all of a sudden it was my truck, but obviously I was going to take the heat for whoever had given him a hard time.

"We catch up to one of your monsters on a straight stretch of two-lane road on '97, north of Williams Lake. It's raining and there's a pile of spray coming off all those wheels. He's loaded to the moon with lumber, so I have to cross into the other lane to see what's coming. I can see the driver's arm waving me to pass him, so I pull out into the spray and start crawling by him."

"Jcez!" he rants on. "This truck has two loaded trailers and has to be five or six car lengths long. I've got the gas pedal to the floor and I'm barely creeping by when I see lights coming at us. If that truck hadn't slowed down to let me back into my own lane, it could have been curtains! They've got to build those trucks shorter so motorists can pass safely!"

"Darn straight!" I reply, trying to keep from grinning but also trying to keep the peace. Truth is, I've seen Orv's car and his driving. Trucker's nightmare! He's got one of these four-cylinder Japanese jobs with the same torque as an egg beater. His gas pedal has never been near the floorboard, and he white-knuckles the steering wheel, just holding the speed limit.

That hi-miler with the Super B load of lumber probably saved Orv's scrawny neck by braking to let him in, but this seemed like a poor time to bring it up. Anyway, after getting all this off his chest, he wandered off, leaving me wondering just why were our rigs getting so enormous?

Over the last forty years I got to watch them grow, and Orville has a point.

If he figured they look big from the outside, he should sit behind the tiller where we are and try to see the back end of a Super B or a set of triples through your "go-backwards."

Ever pull a set of A-trains, guys? First advice you were ever given was "Don't watch the rear trailer in your mirror. It's too scary."

Oops! I'm wandering away from the story.

Our present day mileage merchants will never believe that most trucking done in the 1960s was done with single-axle tractors and a pair of twenty-six-foot trailers. That was the way until a few years ago. The guys in suits will tell you that rigs got bigger because of demand and competition, but I have another theory.

It's because the other guy had a bigger one.

So help me, I watched it happen. One of the big fleets somewhere started using tandems and first thing you know, the little guys are adding tag axles and pony axles and V-drives to their single-axles. No increase in power or traction, just more freight. Pandemonium!

Those things would spin out on a martini olive, and on an icy hill, they'd decorate the roads and ditches like a field of daisies. I tell you, they were as useless as cardboard cowboy boots.

Thankfully, that madness was short-lived. Tandem-axle

tractors became common and big power reared its ugly head.

Oh, the stunts that drivers would pull to make others believe they had some fire-belching stable under the hood! Slipping a six-inch stack over the four-inch chimney that the truck came with and conning a mechanic into changing the button in your fuel pump had a certain, limited success until the guy who owned the rig totalled up the extra fuel all of a sudden or—gasp!—ended up with a fried engine.

Smoke and noise meant more power, so some desperate skinners would punch out the guts of their mufflers with a steel bar, then drop an oak axe handle down the chimney. When that wood started to burn, there were smoke and sparks and a racket that'd wake up a senator.

Of course, this didn't up the power one little squirt, so it was usually only the guy driving it who was impressed. Eventually, one of the fleets bought tandems with 250-horse Cummins engines and, naturally, the rest followed. I sure remember when the outfit I was with bought its first batch. Going from 185 horses up to 250 was awesome. I figured, "Oh yeah, this is raw power. They'll never get stronger than this!"

With a GVW (gross vehicle weight) of 72,000 pounds, we could fly. Well, colour me short-sighted, because the last time I checked, those engine companies were squeezing in five-hundred-plus palominos and still going. With that kind of power, you can bet your safety bonus that the rigs were going to get bigger.

The day also arrived when fleets were having heartburn trying to attract drivers. The cabs had to become user-friendly, as bait. All those old, solid steel cabs were cramped cold, and rough. The B-model Mack, for example, was so narrow, you could sunburn both arms at once. The rubber block-and-spring suspensions on all the trucks were so stiff that if you hit a pothole, the shock would stop your watch.

Here we went again. If Sam's Winch and Snatch Block Service bought bigger cabs with more power, then Archie's Winch and Boom rushed out and financed a bunch. This was great for the drivers, but now we had to pack heavier loads with bigger trucks to pay for all this pretty tin. We've got to the point now where our hi-cubes and reefers are bigger than boxcars, and our Super B trailers, etc, are so long and heavy that when we arrive at a rail crossing, the train stops to let *us* go by!

You know something? If we now have 500 ponies to pull 140,000 pounds, and it all started with 250 horses pulling 72,000 pounds, we haven't gained all that much, eh gang?

It's our five-star sleeper cabs that have Orville and the public fooled. Our truck cabs haven't got a whole lot bigger, but the manufactures' and owners' competition for the biggest and best sleeper generated some doozies. The average guy figures that's where the engine is or where we carry more freight. They don't realize that if we added a screen door and a porch light, we'd have a freakin' cottage!

Maybe Orville is right. In the meantime, we're stuck with the government story. Still, there's one statistic that'd make Orv happy. If you lined up all the highway trucks in western Canada end to end, 50 per cent of them would pull into the nearest truck stop.

Problem solved!

THE NEW STUFF

YOU'VE GOT TO AGREE, THERE HAVE BEEN SOME fantastic improvements on the big rigs over the last bunch of years. Oh, I know that some of you are thinking, "Great! He's finally thinking clearly. They must have got his medication right." But I really am impressed.

I suppose most of us take the present thundering diesel gobbler for granted, but just pull over in a wide spot for a sec and think about it. When I started hi-miling, the state-of-the-art rig was a cabover Kenworth with a 250-horse Cummins and a four-by-four tranny. We all figured this was as good as it got. How could they improve on this?

Well, colour me ignorant, but the changes were already happening. Every batch of new trucks the company bought came with the most modern do-dads. Some of them were peachy and others were ho-hum or even a pain where your legs join. Now I look at today's rig and wonder where it will all stop.

My second thought (imagine—two thoughts in one day!) was which of these vast improvements was the most important to me. I pondered this for some time.

Was it the increased power? With the horses now double and climbing over my old 250, it's certainly one of the biggies. Matter of fact, I'm convinced they can't stuff too many more horses under one hood. What with Super B's, doubles and triples with all that weight, I think the next step is a pusher at the back, like the pea-pickin' railroads. Ha! Wouldn't that be something to eyeball! Mind you, my old 250 travelled the same roads as today, and with lighter loads, we weren't far behind the bigger engines. What with speed limits, traffic and all, unless you're in a real ball-busting hurry to get somewhere, that increased horsepower was wasted. Nope. I don't think that was the greatest improvement.

How about that Jacobs engine brake? Man, that was a big improvement over the old Williams exhaust brake. For those of you unfamiliar with that goofy device, it was an air-controlled flap that closed over inside the exhaust pipe. I suppose it helped slow the engine down for quicker shifting, but as a downhill retarder, it was useless as a siren on a stroller. You could probably get better results stepping outside and holding your hand over the stack. The Jake brake was designed as a safety feature and brake saver, but as I and all drivers discovered, you could go downhill a lot faster with one of those babies. It may have helped the brakes a little, but thanks to some of the guys who never shut the bloody thing off—even bobtailing—all it really succeeded in doing was annoying the public. No way this thing is my choice.

Power steering. Now we're talking. Ask any white line warrior who had to drive a big rig without it, and he'll tell you that wheeling around city streets or backing trailers into tight spots with standard steering was murder. Drivers' arms ended up thicker and longer than normal. No, really! I remember when power steering first became available and some of the old hands would say, "That's not for me! You can't feel the road." Well, I've got news. After five hundred miles or a day in the city of wrestling that steering wheel, you couldn't feel anything from your shoulders to your little pinkies anyway. Personally, I figured the person who designed power steering for trucks should get a medal. That's still not my number one choice, though.

Radial tires are brilliant! Oh, how we all hated bias rubber with inner tubes. If you only had two flats in an eight hundred-mile trip, she was a complete success. The only good thing about stopping once an hour to thump all eighteen was that we never developed bladder problems. As a matter of fact, finding a flat was lucky because if it went flat on the move, and that stupid inner tube valve stem slipped inside, it would chew up the tire in minutes and get hot enough to catch fire shortly after. We spent as much time watching our mirrors for smoke as we did staring out the windshield. Mind you, like you modern guys, we also watched cars passing us, hoping they'd be full of naked girls, but I never even saw one like that. Those tubeless radials are great, but I'm still undecided.

Big sleepers. Oh, lordy! I'd have killed for one of those ballroom-sized bunks you see nowadays. Engine controls,

TV sets, storage space. Would you believe a thirty-inch wide bunk in those old cabovers served as home for weeks on end, with two drivers living in that tin hotel? Storage space was almost nil, so with spare parts and our travel bags, we must have looked like a gypsy wagon. Ask a guy to drive one of those now, and you'd get the centre finger salute. Those big bunks are a great invention, but I'm still thinking.

Well, leaping line-haulers! I think I've got it!

Air conditioning.

Big deal, you say? Well, turn yours off and keep reading, my skeptical buddy. As we all know, those big diesel-drinking engines generate a ton of heat. Cabover or conventional, we're sitting right next to it, and without insulation, it'd be hotter than a skidoo suit in a sauna. I suspect good insulation was hard to come by years ago, and air conditioning was too expensive to slap into your run-of-the-mill fleet truck. I suppose we welcomed the heat in winter because generally the cab heaters were on a par with rubbing two sticks together. For some reason, those old cabovers had huge windshields, so the piddly little heat we could generate all had to go up the defroster to keep the glass clear. I wish I'd taken pictures of drivers with blankets wrapped around them to convince you.

Look out when summer arrived! Talk about climate controlled. In the winter we froze, and in the summer we fried. I still get sweaty thinking of crawling up long hills with that engine belching heat, and the hot summer sun beaming through all that glass, with no breeze and us sitting in our Stanfields, stuck to those freakin' leather seats.

Memories of one particular trip helped me put air

conditioning at the top of my list. My co-pilot, Nicky, and I had wound our way along Highway 3, through the Kootenays in southern BC one hot fall day, and by the time we dropped down into the resort town of Osoyoos, we were darn near demised.

That highway runs right alongside a beach and lake, which was just what the doctor ordered. All we had on were our Fruit of the Looms, but this end of the beach looked deserted, so we were out and into the water in a blur. We weren't in that water more than two minutes when a bus pulls up behind our rig and unloads a whole flock of school kids, all wearing swim suits. Our fate was sealed. If Nicky and I bolted out of there in our undies, we'd probably get arrested as perverts and more than likely would have got twenty years. So we headed for deeper water and waited it out.

Luckily, the kids had a tight schedule and split an hour later. We streaked to our truck, looking like big, white raisins. It was the one time we appreciated that rubber mounted oven. You see? One lousy little air conditioner would have prevented all that hassle.

I close with the immortal words of the guy who owned the trucks still ringing in my ears.

"Air conditioning in a truck? It'll never happen!"

TIN CAVE

I'M WALKING ALONG ONE OF THE MAIN STREETS IN Vancouver with a non-trucking buddy of mine awhile back, when a real classy rig rumbles slowly by. It's a middle-aged conventional with inch-thick paint and polish, an identical-colour stripe running the length of the tri-axle "fridge" he's pulling, and the reflection off the chrome is bright enough to start a fire. It's got a walk-in sleeper the size of a temple.

"Whoa, nice rig," I say. "Did you see it?"

"A truck is a truck," my friend says.

Well, you could have knocked me over with a used fuel filter! I knew my friend was no big truck fan, but we were talking "work of art" here. My fellow graduates of Gear Masher U would have strung him up from the nearest lamp post upon hearing this, but I put his lack of appreciation down to a poor and unhappy childhood.

What young kid wouldn't have pumped an arm in the air when a "boss rig" like that moaned by? I stopped shaking my head, stood fully erect (which was no big deal, at five-foot ten, with full heels on my Boulet boots). I looked him in the eye.

"Gordie, Gordie," I says. "There are scads of different trucks. You see lots of trucks with gravel boxes, right? They may or may not be state-of-the-art rigs, but how far are you going to haul gravel? Most of those trucks barely get out of sight. You also see some pretty classy 'iron' pulling trailers around town, but they have back windows in their cabs, so you know darn well they'll be home for supper. It's the bedroom at the back, Gordie—the sleeper—that puts trucks like that at the top of the list. You know, white-line fever, king-of-the-road stuff."

He grins back at me.

"Who cares?"

Well, I'd tried, but you can't convert them all.

I'm still impressed by fancy rigs and still check the decals to see where they hail from. Lots of folks have asked me what it's like hurling down the highway, lying in that bunk. The first thing I tell them is that if you're running solo, having that bunk is a gift. It has all the comforts of a hotel room, except plumbing. When the rig is parked, you can sleep like a baby. When you're team driving, though, it's a whole different can of beans. The nearest way to feel the experience of lying in a moving bunk goes like this:

Stretch out on the floor beside your clothes dryer at home, and set it to run for six hours. Get someone to shake you gently the whole time and pull you down a couple of inches by your feet every once in awhile to imitate going around a corner too fast. You can ask your shaker to swear occasionally to indicate a driver problem. That's about as close as I can come to what it's like.

Truth of the matter is that it takes a lot of practice to sleep under those conditions, and not everyone who attempts it is successful. I've teamed with a few guys who were on their virgin trips and fell out of the cab, after a five-day rounder, with bags under their eyes the size of spuds and eyeballs the colour of muscatel. I, on the other hand, had no trouble sleeping at all, and enjoyed the team driving like crazy.

There were some funny moments involving those tin motels, some of which I've already shared with you. There was poor old Tiny, who got trapped in one, and Sparky, who would lie back there, plotting ways to screw me up in his practical-joking way. One of his "faves" was reaching out to steal a shift stick in our cabover Kenworth—with the good old four-and-four trannies—causing me much scrambling on the way up a hill. That twisted swine!

The one bunk experience that scared me more than a tax audit happened in a mountain pass in BC. A sixth sense that most team drivers acquire woke me up, because it was quiet when it shouldn't have been. I peeked out the curtain and discovered that the spareboard driver with me had the truck out of gear, and we were flying like a thirty-five-ton spear down the south side of the Salmo-Creston cutoff. In the headlights, I noticed us zip by one of the many emergency pulloffs.

"Good grief!" I thought. "This guy must figure those trails are for the moose!"

As calmly as I could, I looked over at the smiling driver, mentioned that this hill was almost the length of North America and ended at a "T," paralleling the very cold Columbia River, where we had to make a tight right turn. I slipped back into the bunk and just lay there, laughing at all the people I owed money to, knowing they'd never see a dime after this!

A lurch and rubber squeal indicated that my friend was standing on the brake pedal and a roar told me that the engine had come to life and we were back in gear. Moments later, I ended up in a ball at one end of the sleeper, but apparently he had made it around the corner and we were still moving, just a little less than the speed of light.

Well, being adults, and macho men of the world, we couldn't actually show fear, so we both sat quietly, white as a nurse's nylons, staring out the windshield.

Another sleeper story that always gave me a chuckle was about an old hand by the name of Murray. He was one of those million milers and was always a real pleasure to team with. He did have one unusual quirk, however—his eyelids would roll open as he slept. For those of us who knew about this, it was no big deal, but for a first-timer looking in on him, it could be quite a shock. Not only would he be staring back at you, but because he was a sound sleeper, it usually took a fair amount of noise or shaking to wake him up.

One of the spare-boarders who drew a trip with Murray damn near died before his time. He pulls into a truck stop, opens the curtain to wake Murray, and there's the guy, staring straight up at the padded headliner. The spareboarder gives Murray a little shake, to no avail, and then he loses it. He bails out of the cab, hollers at the station attendant to call an ambulance, and grabs a phone to call the Edmonton dispatcher.

"Murray is dead!" he hollers. "He died in the bunk!"

Luckily, the dispatcher was aware of Murray's little eyelid thing and finally calmed the guy down. To top it off, Murray walks up to the guy while he's still on the phone, and this immediately put the Nervous Nelly back on course.

The dispatchers made a point of telling anyone who ran with Murray after that about this little problem. There was always the fear that someone would look in on the guy on the move and panic. Then Murray would probably die for real.

The last goofy bunk experience I must pass along also involves the dispatchers and a guy we called Moe. For some unknown reason, he would usually come out of the sleeper swinging his fists. It was as if he felt he was under attack or was just plain angry. It only lasted a minute or two. Then he would calm down and apologize like crazy to the poor schnook who got pulverized. Other than this anti-social arousal pattern, the guy was great. He was funny and relaxed, believe it or not.

Anyway, the only safe way to wake him up at shift change was to get out of the cab, beat on the side of the sleeper, and step back. He was usually pleasant and quiet, like a funeral usher, but the dispatchers made a major point of warning the new guys about Moe.

I'd better stop right there, because I'm making those sleepers out to be chambers of horrors. Nothing could be further from the truth, and I sure don't want to spook the up-and-coming tin cave dwellers. Remember, gang, we're paid by the mile, so waking up three hundred miles down the road is like free money.

Nighty-night!

RUNAWAY

SHE'S FUELED UP, WASHED DOWN, LOOKED OVER, hooked to a wagon and ready for me to climb aboard and cut 'er loose.

Do I think of brakes at this point?

Not likely, Liz!

The wrench-yankers have given her a clean bill of health. She's got more bells and backup systems than a nuke reactor, and I've got an air endorsement on my Class One.

Buddy, I'm paid to go, not stop!

Besides, what could possibly go wrong?

Oopsy! Famous last words.

Truth is, not a whole heck of a lot can go wrong, long as we don't get 'em too hot. We all know glazed brakes act like a banana skin on a boot bottom. Of course, there are always those scary-looking runoff roads waiting for you alongside most steep hills. That could wreck your whole day, burying Old Fang in one of those plowed up patches!

Point of all this babble is that brakes on eighteen-wheelers weren't always as safe and dependable as they are today. In my humble opinion, brakes were improved over the years just as fast as something failed on the oldies. The old "iron" we herded awhile back didn't have the likes of air dryers, maxi-brakes or plastic lines. Our air dryer was a bottle of methyl alcohol, and our maxi-brake was a rubber gasket in a valve. Air lines were rubber, which cracked when it got cold and rotted any old time.

Believe me, we went down most hills the same speed we could climb them—freakin' slow! Even some of the hills and mountain passes were eventually improved after a few big rigs tore up the scenery.

Far be it from old Donny to turn this into a history lesson, because those same hills are still there for you guys. Mind you, with today's engine retarders and state-of-the-art anchors, what was a heart-thumping grade to us is probably a flight path for you.

I'll bet you a chrome sun visor that there are still some of those butt-squeezing mountain passes out there that still demand a little respect. One that leaps to mind, although it's been vastly improved, is the Trans Canada Highway through Kamloops in a BC mountain valley.

Actually, the city got tired of smoking trucks screaming through town, so years ago they built a bypass highway. We were all happy as a puppy in a room full of slippers when they completed that baby! Eastbound, skirting Kamloops, you still drop like a crowbar in a creek for fifteen or twenty miles, but it's a whole lot straighter and gentler than the old through-town route.

I did both roads more times than I care to think about, and all I suffered were hemorrhoids from the close calls. That old route through the city fueled a ton of truck stories, and the one I always recall happened to a couple of buddies of mine running double on a cabover Kenworth—the sister of Old Fang.

Lyle in the pilot seat, headed east with Al in the bunk, started down into the Big K early one winter morning. It was plenty cold, and blacker than a coal miner's hanky, but the road was dry and traffic was almost non-existent.

The first few miles of grade were fairly gentle, so Lyle was pretty well letting the rig roll, until the halfway point, where the hill got steeper as he started to apply more brake. According to the gauges, he was pumping and applying lots of wind, but the old girl wasn't slacking off. Up until now, everything had been working fine, but now something had taken a dive.

Lyle and Al had both trucked in the oil patch, had years of hi-miling and had pretty well seen it all. But—oh, brother! —what was coming up darn few of us have ever experienced. The rest of this ski jump—about four miles of it—gets increasingly steeper, ending with a half-mile long, curvy chunk going almost straight down into town.

By the time they reached that point, Lyle had thrown the truck out of gear to save the engine from self-destructing, had the brake pedal mashed to the floor and was gripping the wheel like a Scotsman holding his train fare. The Sangamo tachometer mounted above the doghouse—with a top reading of eighty-five MPH—had the needle clicking at that spot, trying for a higher number.

That's what Al saw when he stuck his head out of the bunk to complain about the rough ride and wisely disappeared again.

One of the Queen's Finest took after this bullet as it blew by him on the main street, but with Lyle's head start, he didn't have a hope. The road levels off at this point, but the worst was yet to come. At the far end of town, the highway does a forty-five-mile-an-hour "S" curve, and the rig is still going ballistic.

Thanks to a load of steel bars with a low centre of gravity, Lyle has already defied the engineers' calculations around a couple of corners, but now what? Luckily, we're talking residential along here, so the buildings were set well away from the road.

Cool as you please, Lyle plows over the curb and onto a snow-covered lawn, clipping a corner of the house on his left side. Then he careens back over the highway and shows the same disrespect to the yard and house on the other side, where he clips off the ditch-side mirror in the process. But at least he's still on his Firestones and has dropped below the speed of sound.

This last house gets a rock garden trashed and fifteen feet of back picket fence is history, but—stone the seagulls!—old Lyle clunks back onto the highway, which is now flat and straight as a suit salesman's pleat. That sucker rolls for another mile or so and finally comes to rest. Lyle just sits there, with that white-knuckle grip on the wheel, staring out the windshield. He doesn't even move when the cop, who came in second, knocks on the door. Al peeks out of the sleeper, assuming it's Saint Peter doing the knocking, and is amazed to discover that they both survived!

To cut to the chase (so to speak), some frozen crud in the valves had apparently caused the problem. A thorough inspection the next day showed all was up to snuff except for oily air lines. Lyle went home to Edmonton on the bus from Kamloops and never drove truck again. I'm told crazy Al still sniffs "glad hands" to this day, checking for oily air.

PART FOUR

MOUNTAINS AND
MINOR OBSTACLES

CLIMB ABOARD

'M SURE MY FELLOW WAGON YANKERS WILL AGREE
that the most-often-asked question about trucking is
"How does it feel when you lose control?" These curious
folks hardly ever ask about fuel consumption, gross weight,
rules and regulations, or how's the wife and kids. Oh, no! It's
always how our latest near-disaster went. I've got it figured
that so much media attention is paid to rigs that run into a
spot of trouble that everyone is convinced we lose 'er twice
a day or are never in complete control at all.

Well, I think the only way to put that twisted concept to
bed is to document one of my trips and try to convey what
we do for a living. Hey, it's worth a try. Like they say in mar-
keting, let's peel it and see if it squirts. So let's assume we're
showing a reporter how it really is. Here's how it might go.

The only way to demonstrate what happens is to take
you along on a trip, so you, dear civilian, had better zip

around to the ditch side, climb into the jump seat, throw your bag into the sleeper, buckle up, and keep your bleepin' feet off the dashboard. If you touch any buttons or levers without asking me first, I'll get really cranky.

Now remember, it's the middle of winter. We're headed for Vancouver, eight hundred miles away from here in Edmonton, and if you look in the go-backwards, you'll see that we're pulling a forty-five-foot flatdeck, loaded with twenty-four tons of steel bars. Yeah, yeah. I know it's cold and noisy, but this is a big cab, and it takes a few minutes to heat. You'll get used to the noise. Matter of fact, if the racket quits while we're still moving, it's a sure sign I'm about to earn my money, as we'll be on ice.

You're right—I'm shifting gears with this long metal rod, and the more times I do it, the faster we go, so quit bouncing around, just in case there's ice on the highway under all this bleeping snow. Why don't you climb into the sleeper and try to get some rest? It's flatter than a plywood guitar from here through Calgary and all the way to Banff. I promise to wake you if I roll the rig between here and there, so you can feel the experience.

Well, hi there! No, no—relax! The engine went quiet because we're at a stop sign in Calgary. Go back to the coffin—oops—I mean, the bunk, and I'll wake you at Valley Gap, where we stop to graze. Yes, correct—that'll be for supper. (Good grief! Bleepin' rookie!)

Yup, that's Field Hill ahead, the one we have to crawl down. No, actually, all this snow helps traction. We just have to take it slow in case there's ice under it. No, I wasn't counting tires at the Gag and Heave back there. I know there are eighteen. I was checking for flats. No, they don't go "floppa, floppa" like a car. These get hot and catch fire sometimes. Yeah, really! No, that truck driver stopped halfway up the hill isn't dead. He's lying on the road, doing up his tire chains. I told you this was a goofy way to make a living!

Oh, by the way, you'll be interested to know that we're basically out of control now. If the fur ball has hit the fan further down, our chances of stopping this rig are the same as getting a pork chop through a dog pound.

Okay, we're on flat road again. You can take your hands away from your eyes now. Hold on! There's a moose on the road.

Sorry about that! Yeah, it scares me, too. We got lucky, though. He jumped back into the snow bank. Sometimes they figure the truck is a trespassing rival or something, and they charge us. Those critters weigh a ton and can do a whole passle of damage. Damn straight! Those bright landing lights help us see a long way ahead.

Listen, my friend—you try to get another forty winks. I'm going to pull over in Golden, up the road a bit and slump over the wheel for a couple of hours before we start through Rogers Pass. No worries! I'll wake you up when we start to climb. I know, it's tough to sleep with all this rockin' and roarin', but you've got a few hours anyway.

You're right! It looks like a feather factory out there. Been snowing like that since Golden. I'll bet a buck to a pinch of raccoon poo that we have to chain up to climb the Pass. I doubt the plows can keep up to this mess. Yeah, I know it's cold in here. We have to keep the heat off the windshield so that the snow won't melt and then freeze up the wipers. No, I'm not scared. I do this trip twice a week. Relax!

Okay, we're coming up to the first climb of Rogers Pass, and—oh, ratburgers!—the chain-up sign is showing. If I didn't have you along this trip, I might have ignored the sign because it's pretty cold and traction is good, but not tonight. You stay put. I'm just going to drape the jewellry over one axle. And by the way, those buttons are coloured red and yellow to warn passengers not to touch them while I'm out of the cab.

There! I told you, it only takes a sec. Now I flip this diff lock switch—no, no—I don't have to see it. I know where all the switches are, so I don't have to take my eyeballs off the road. Yeah, it's going to be rough riding and slow going like this until we reach the summit. Sit down, we aren't spinning out. The old girl is just wiping her feet a little. It'll happen every once and awhile.

I can't see the road either, but I know where it is.

What happens if the tire chains break? Oh, let me see— we'll probably slide backwards for a bit, then we'll make some really amazing patterns in the snow all over the road. Eventually, the truck and trailer will form a capital L." Then it'll soar off the side of the mountain like a forty-ton turkey.

There, are you happy now? Quit with the negative thoughts, already! This truck and I have been through worse than this. I know when it's time to jump.

Get your hand off the door handle!

Just kidding. I'll stop at the Summit Coffee Shop. Hold it until then and we'll get something to eat too.

Okay, here we go. I feel better too. That used oil they called coffee back there should keep me awake for hours. Going down this side of the Pass can get a little hairy. I have to keep gearing up at the right times, to keep our wagon behind us instead of alongside, so we'll end up going a little faster than we should. If you're going to stay up and watch, promise me you won't look in the mirror. I've got to concentrate on a whole handful of things, so keep the screaming down to a minimum.

Whoa, girl! Whoa! That's it . . . that's it . . . whew! Tight corner.

Climb, baby, climb! Oops! No feet-wiping. I'll slack off, old girl. Just get us down this next grade, and I promise I'll buy you a wash job in Vancouver. Atta girl!

Well, there you go. That's the worst five hours of the whole trip. We came as close to losing it as darn is to swearing. When the trailer swings out like that, only sheer luck puts it back where it should be.

That's Revelstoke coming up. It's getting warmer out already, and you can see it's stopped snowing. You can let go of the dashboard now and let the blood back into your fingers. No, I'm not real tired yet. That run through the Pass winds me up higher than Sputnik. I'll pull over in Sicamous so we can get some vittles, and I'll count the tires again. Then I'll crash—oops! I mean "rest"—there for a couple hours. We still have the Fraser Canyon to face, and it can be a mite dicey.

Well, I'll be whooped! You finally woke up! That means you're used to the rumble and the roar. You slept right through Kamloops and Cache Creek, so Fraser Canyon, here we come!

What? Oh, sure. I'll pull over in a minute, and you can powder your nose beside the rig. I've got to stretch the legs anyway.

Here we go again, and no, don't worry about running out of gas. Firstly, we burn diesel, and second, we carry three hundred gallons of the stuff, which is enough to get us to Vancouver. Man, you're lucky this trip! We're going through here in daylight. This has got to be the world's worst road for black ice. We're getting closer to the Pacific Ocean and to warmer weather, so the high spots like Jackass and American Mountain thaw during the day and freeze over again at night. You just never know when it switches. No problems today, though.

That's the other thing we have to watch for. No, it's not smoke, it's fog or low clouds. No, that's not a radar machine. It's called a "stool pigeon," and it's recording all the things the truck is doing.

I can't see the road either. That's why we're crawling. But I can see the line beside me and I know exactly where we are. Calm down. The other skinners are going as slow as I am.

Aha! It's starting to rain! Our next stop is Hope for lunch. Then just two hours into Vancouver.

Well, did you enjoy the trip? I agree! It's hard to believe it was minus-thirty when we left the Big Onion. Yeah, I know. You decided to fly home. No problem! Just think of me as you zoom over the Rocky Mountains, will you? Hey, you're welcome!

Well, gang, other than a rhumba dance coming off the Summit, we were in control the whole time. Point is, the only time we totally lose control is when we're Christmas shopping, just like everyone else.

TRUCKERS BEWARE

PULL 'ER OVER AND PARK 'ER, BOYS. AS I WRITE this in mid-March, it just snowed in Vancouver.

There's only a couple of inches so far, but it's already pan-dee-moan-eum. She's coming down like wet concrete, with flakes the size of flapjacks, and the bald-tire brigade is on the streets in full force. I'll bet you a set of new Freightliner mud-flaps we're going to get a foot or better, which means close the city and turn off the lights.

Now, that tandem-axle, fire-belching, mobile motel of yours would have no trouble at all getting around with a set of singles on for "gription," but every other vehicle on the city streets—including the People's Transit System—runs on treadless slicks. In the time it takes you to remember where you stowed your Oilfield Oxfords (rubber boots), the inter-sections are all shined up like a politician's smile.

Will someone please explain to dumb, old Donny here,

how a Vancouver motorist can mash the gas pedal when the light turns green—or whatever his favourite colour is—then set the speedometer needle at eighty klicks and never bother to look out the window to see he ain't moving? Picture thousands of these pavement polishers, all whirling at the same time and we're talking kay-OSS! It's only been snowing for an hour, dumping maybe two inches max, and already most city roads are at a standstill.

The problem now is not the four wheelers who can't get rolling, it's the ones who did! They still come charging up to the intersection like they usually do and expect the family beater to stop on a dime, even if the road looks like a mirror. They sift into whatever unlucky vehicles are in the way, turning the street into an auto wrecker's paradise. At this point, you're on your own, Orville, because the tow trucks and the law can't get to you. Even the insurance company and the body shops tell you to take a number and call in a week or two!

The way I see it, there are two major factors which turn Vancouver into a circus when it snows. Number one is location. Downtown Vancouver is just a shade above sea level, although during heavy winter rainstorms it appears to be a foot or two below. The rest of the village clings to the side of the mountains.

The point is, if you're heading from downtown Vancouver to Japan, you've got a fairly flat ride, but any other direction out of town and you've gotta climb. Practically every street within city limits has hills in it, and a snow storm turns them all into six-lane ski jumps.

The second problem is that snow doesn't happen here much. Most winters in this land-of-salmon-and-senior-citizens may have snow on the ground lasting ten to fourteen days max, and some winters have none at all. So nobody gets much practice driving in snow.

We do have lots of skiers here, of course, who strap on their Honda Civics or SUVs and race each other to the many ski hills up in the mountains. Although their four-wheelers are better-equipped for snow than most city cars, they tend to drive like they ski, bashing into each other and littering the roads out of town with demolished imports.

The budget for the city snow problem can be a crapshoot also. City Hall appears to set aside about forty-seven dollars for snow removal and about four billion for salt. I think the policy is this—for every two inches of snow that falls, they spread four inches of salt. Three hours of snowing and salting leaves you driving through axle-deep oatmeal.

The real movie-making areas are the really steep hills, where even the salt-flingers can't climb and which are simply barricaded top and bottom with a "Road Closed" sign tacked on. Well, this attracts the weekend warriors, with their four-wheel drive pickups. They firmly believe the salesman who claimed they could climb walls with these vehicles.

The ones who come down from the top usually hit warp speed before taking out the bottom barricade and joining the mangled mess in the intersection. The really smart ones start from the bottom, usually get part way up, reach over for another beer and turn the tiller far enough to lose whatever traction their fancy Datsun had. They do a couple of 360s, one or two curb-to-curb bounces, and if they're lucky, end up on some guy's lawn. The unlucky ones twirl all the way back down to the bottom, joining their buddies at the body parts sale in the intersection.

By now, this winter wonderland is a foot deep or better and nobody is going anywhere. The hotels are doing a booming business, and the bars are standing-room only because you can't get home. Eventually, the city snowplows descend on the scene, but by then most of the streets have become parking lots for abandoned cars. The plows push the oatmeal to the side as best they can, plugging up the curb drains and blocking in any poor schmuck who stayed parked in the first place.

If it continues to snow, off in the distance you hear the gentle snap of trees breaking under the weight of this white wonder. They fall across roads and cars, and oops!—there go the house lights. I guess the wires are coming down or some Speedy Gonzalez has just extricated a power pole. Wait a minute! What was that crunching sound? Oh. The flat roof on that bowling alley just collapsed.

I'll probably lose my tee-off time tomorrow morning.

Ratburgers!

Now you see why I recommended that you park Old Fang on the outskirts of the city for the night. She's nuts in here, boys, and you're hearing this from an old pro. I did years of wagon-draggin' through this city and survived half a dozen winters that I'd rather forget.

Before that, I called Edmonton home for years and lived with True Canadian Winters, with snow on the roads six months of the year, but I never experienced there what I saw in the Big V. It's no pea-pickin' wonder that the rest of Canada giggles when snow hits the coast. This zoo is unique. Even the rest of the province contends with the annual Canadian deep freeze, but it appears that as soon as someone enters the city limits, they take off their snow tires, turn their caps backwards, and forget all they learned about winter wheeling.

For truckers who get stuck in this traffic madness, the windshield becomes a TV screen. We sit up in our warm commander air ride, overtop this mechanical mess and watch the performance.

I've been stopped in a lineup of vehicles where the brake lights stretched as far as the eye could see and nothing was moving. The main drag, a six-lane road, has been reduced to two lanes, one east and one west. Deep snow down the middle and abandoned cars on the ditch sides determine the lanes.

I take a peek in my go-backwards, and damned if the car right behind me doesn't pull out from behind the loaded B-train I'm pulling and try to pass me! Well, leapin' Jesus!

There's oncoming traffic crawling along, and this brain surgeon pulls out right in front of them! Then he gets halfway into their lane and high centres on that middle snow dune. He's got his engine screaming, flat out, but nothing's happening.

Finally he bails out of his beater, empties a bag of something around what he can see of his back wheels, jumps back in, and cranks his engine back up to destruct phase, not realizing he has front wheel drive. The traffic in my lane starts to crawl ahead, and the last I can see as I pull away is this maniac having a fist fight with a couple of guys he's blocked!

Ain't winter motoring grand?

For truckers, there are far more problems than the traffic. By the next day, most of the cars in Vancouver are in a body shop somewhere or stuffed into the carport where they belong. Now the plowed-up snow drifts become the problem. Those right-hand turns with fifty-three feet of semi-trailer are tighter than a Scotsman's tip.

If, by some stretch of the imagination, you get to where you're going, your troubles have just started. Probably Sam's Snow Removal Service has taken the snow from the middle of the shipper's yard and plowed it up against the freight dock. The pile is so high, you won't be able to back in there until spring. Even if the dock is clear, chances are good that the approaches are all piled up, so the only way you can get your hi-cube to the door is to pick it up and carry it over. You can also count on the cargo you're supposed to load being covered in snow. Warehouse? What warehouse? It never snows in Vancouver!

Even if your deck or floor is swept, try lashing ice-covered pallets or what-have-you, tight enough to stay put. I've watched drivers throw belts over a load for an hour and the first corner they turn, they get buried in falling freight.

Most fleet operators in Vancouver have the sense to park the iron at the first sight of snow, and—read my lips,

Reggie!—you'd be real wise to do the same. I'm firmly convinced that there's a sign on the city limits that reads:

WELCOME TO VANCOUVER.

PLEASE LEAVE AT LEAST FOUR INCHES BETWEEN YOUR CAR AND THE VEHICLE YOU ARE FOLLOWING.

DISREGARD POSTED SPEED LIMITS.

Please ignore this sign when you head out here next winter.

WHOA, NELLIE!

AH, KIDS AND QUESTIONS. THEY GO TOGETHER like beans and gas. If you don't take my word for it, just ask any gear-smasher what happens when you park your rig anywhere near a gaggle of parental delights.

"Hey! How come the truck has to be so high?"

"How come you have so many wheels?"

"How come there's so much dead stuff on the front?"

"Did you ever drive to Cornplaster, Manitoba? My sister lives there!"

It's kind of fun, really, because when I first got turned loose with an eighteen-wheeler, I romantically pictured the rig as a huge stagecoach, with me sitting up on top, hollering at eight mighty horses. When you think about it, those old trucks were darn similar to the old-time western wagons. Bone-shaking ride, hot in the summer, cold in the winter and the horses always seemed a little lame.

Oops! Sounds like I never bothered to grow up.

Anyway one of the most often asked questions was, "How fast will your truck go?" I'd usually reply that she could do the speed limit, which didn't impress the kids much when they saw that huge engine and figured we should go like a rocket. I didn't like to bore them with the fact that where we're going and what we're hauling determines how Old Fang is geared and what she'll do flat out. If you're climbing mountains or carrying crawlers, you want the Old Girl strong, not speedy. If you're hauling Kleenex to Kenora, you can afford to give her longer legs.

Those are bare facts and all, but I'll bet every hi-miler has the same daydreams I've had. You're cruising across the Prairies or any other flat stretch late at night, with the traffic sparse and the wind at your back. You're in the top notch, with the engine just a hair short of the governor, and no matter how fast you're going, you're wishing you could speed up a little.

Driving company trucks designed to climb mountains with the dazzling top speed of sixty-two miles per hour caused me to dream plenty. It was always so frustrating to be on a straight stretch, where you could safely go ballistic, but even though you were pushing the fuel pedal with both feet, the trucks loaded with cornflakes would pass you like you were standing still.

Actually, the company I drove for did have one extremely fast Autocar tractor and there were piles of great stories about it. The owner was real touchy about speeding and the few old hands who got to drive it were constantly warned about using the top gears. The owner threatened to regear the old girl if he found out someone had tried to get it airborne. Rumour was that it would do over one hundred miles per hour, but nobody had the fixtures to find out.

Funniest episode I recall is the owner getting a phone call one evening from Big Al in Quincey, Idaho. He was eastbound from Seattle, driving the "Big A." Seems he'd been arrested by the highway patrol for speeding and this was the one call he was allowed. No way he could afford his own bail, so he was begging for help.

Sam listens patiently to Big Al.

Then he says, "Okay, relax, Al. Lemme speak to the cop."

An officer comes onto the phone. Sam introduces himself and then asks how fast Al had been clocked at. When he heard the answer, the old man went red as a Mountie's tunic.

"Let him rot!" he hollered, and slammed down the phone.

Would you believe, he let Big Al simmer in that cell for three days before he finally figured he needed the truck and bailed him out!

We figured for sure the tranny would get changed this time, but the very next trip out, one of the guys used it to clear timber off the side of Stevens Pass, and the only things undamaged were the driver and that tranny. End of problem.

Well, you can paint me pansy if you want to, but I was usually happy enough to go whatever speed the rig or the law allowed. Matter of fact, the few lousy times I threw caution to the wind, I usually scared the crap out of myself. One such episode happened awhile back when I was hauling logs in central BC.

We had started clearing a new area, and I had never been over this gravel trail before. To make matters worse, we were coming out loaded over a different road than we went in empty on, so I didn't even get a preview peek. As usual, I had loaded as many logs as the equipment could hold and headed back.

Less than an hour out, I started down what appeared to be a bottomless hill. It was the middle of summer, the road was narrow but acceptable, and I was in the middle of nowhere, so traffic didn't exist. I was taking it pretty shady, not knowing what to expect, but I began to think it would take a week to get this load to the mill at the speed I was going.

I clicked on my radio, asked if anyone in range had been down this hill near the So-and-So Ranch, and old Quinney came right back to me.

"You're on Skinny's Hill. Kick 'er out and give 'er hell! You've got a real steep climb on the other side. Road's pretty straight. No sweat!"

Well, kicking my truck out of gear and letting it roll freely was something I usually avoided, especially when it weighed over 100,000 pounds. And being top-heavy, it rocked from side to side like a box car on a bad track.

I finally decided, "What the heck. Quinney's an old hand." And besides, I'd seen some of the hills we were expected to climb, so taking a run at one that even old Quinney called steep seemed in order.

So I slip Big Red out of gear, let her roll and enjoy the quiet as the engine idles and a cooling breeze wafts through my open windows. Five minutes later, I figure I'm pretty close to the end of this gravel ski jump, and off in the distance I can see part of the hill I'll have to climb.

"Ha!" I'm laughing to myself, smug as hell. I'm doing just under a million miles an hour, so I'll probably have to put my brakes on just to slow down at the top of the stupid hill.

Seconds later, my day takes a dive. Through the trees ahead, I can see the bottom of the hill, complete with a creek running under a very narrow, one-lane, short, steel bridge. Not only is it going to be like threading a needle to stuff this rig into that narrow chute, but the bridge is a shade higher than the road, and that ramp up is going to launch me for sure.

A whole load of thoughts come to mind in a split second. The major one is this load of logs. Most folks probably don't know—or care, for that matter—that we don't tie these loads down to the rig. Basically, gravity holds the trees on the truck and the bark and jiggling lock them together like a box full of kittens in a warm kitchen.

In other words, slamming the brakes on is not an option. The logs tend to leave the trailer and join you in the cab.

My second thought is that any braking at all might force the trailer sideways a smidge in this loose gravel, and at this moment, staying in a very straight line and aiming this rig like a fifty-ton arrow is major-important.

My third thought is to wonder what happened to "Skinny" that they named this hill after him, and last thought—I remember that Quinney's truck always looked beat up.

No bloody wonder!

At any rate, there was no time to analyze any of this, as I hit that sucker at sixty MPH-plus, and I didn't see the bridge so much as feel it pass under me. First the steering axle—then the tractor wheels—then the trailer group. They all took turns going airborne and crashing back to Earth in a cloud of dust, bark, and flying gravel.

Jeez! I didn't even get a chance to check for damage or learn to breathe again because now I'm part-way up a hill with roughly the same grade as a wall. I'm back in gear and shifting down as fast as my sweaty palm can handle.

I crawl over the top just as Quinney comes back on the radio.

"Hey, Maymac 14—take it easy over the narrow bridge at the bottom!"

You ask how fast my truck will go?

Believe me, sonny. You don't want to know!

PEA-PICKIN' MIRACLES

I'M SITTING IN A QUIET SPOT IN HAWAII, THINKING how lucky I am to have such a sweet place to unload a major chunk of the coin I made driving truck (cackle, cackle). I'm also thinking how lucky I was to live long enough to see this place, considering that close calls in our line of work are a regular hassle. The only explanation that my fellow gear-smackers and I have for surviving some of these pickles is that it's pure pea-pickin' miracles.

Set your hamburger down for a sec and think of the times your rig is no longer doing what you want it to, even with your—ahem—driving skills, luck, and some screaming out loud. You're sailing into an obvious disaster when, for some unexplained reason, your wagon gets back behind you where it should be, or the moose jumping out in front of you decides not to fight your Freightliner and disappears into the ditch.

Miracles, boys!

We've all suffered these heart-stoppers, and if you're ahead of schedule and can spare a few minutes, I'd love to lay a few on ya that I made it through as well as a couple of humdingers that my company cohorts put up with.

I mentioned in one of my earlier babblings about flying down a long hill in the Rocky Mountains, doing just under a million miles an hour and hitting black ice just minutes before a forty-five-MPH curve at the bottom was going to launch me into the Fraser River a couple hundred feet down. You tell me that sand truck that showed up at the bottom and turned my lane into a beach was no miracle? Buddy, I thought it was.

Another unexplained beauty happened one winter day in Saskatchewan. Million Mile Sparky and I were headed for Regina out of Vancouver, and a prairie snow storm had just cleared. For those lucky folks who have never seen the Canadian prairies after a snow storm, the best description is a sheet being thrown over the whole world. The prairies are already flatter than a Swedish pancake, and the snow levels the fields, ditches, and roads for as far as your peekers can see. I swear, on a sunny morning like this one, you could see to the next planet.

Anyway, we're plugging along east on the Trans Canada with me in the control booth and Sparky in the jump seat telling a lie about something. God, I loved running with that guy! Even his bull durham was entertaining.

Off in the distance to our left, we could see a black dot with a snow cloud behind it, heading south. It sort of looked like a raisin in a plate of milk. As we get closer to the raisin, it starts to take the shape of a pickup truck, and it's doing warp speed toward our highway.

The Spark and I have been down this road often enough to know there's no highway intersection anywhere near here, so that flying raisin has to be on one of the zillion country dirt roads. Or snow roads, in this case.

We're still a mile or two from crossing this guy's path when Sparky stops mid-baloney.

"Stop the rig!" he yells.

Now I've been this guy's second driver long enough to know not to question his order, and I put the brakes to our cabover Kenworth. We haven't even come to a complete stop when that pickup-turned-fighter-plane hurls across the highway a few feet in front of us and disappears in a cloud of snow down what we assume is more country road. Painfully aware that this nut would have T-boned us if I hadn't stopped, I asked Sparky how he knew to throw out the anchor.

"You won't believe me," he says, "but I smelled trouble and that was the only thing around that could do any damage."

Strange thing is, I figured that this two-tone, dark blue, K-wobbler would stand out in this world of white like a fully-dressed nun at a nudist colony. Maybe that screwball had a death wish and good old Sparky blew his timing.

I've gotta tell ya another mind blower that happened to a couple of our old hands. Hydraulic Jack—a great nickname for a big, tough guy—was eastbound through Banff

Park with Chrome Stack in the sleeper when an oncoming four-wheeler crossed into his lane.

Jack hit the binders at the same time the rig was dipping into a frost heave, and it was just enough jolt to shift part of the twenty-two-ton load of steel pipe he was pulling. The top tiers slid and pipe roared through the sleeper, just barely clearing Chrome Stack and stopping just short of Jack.

Bad as this was, another problem had just started. As that pipe moved ahead, it was doubling the weight on the front end, and it was now pressing down on Chrome Stack so hard that he was trapped and could barely breathe.

Jack bounded out of the cab, cranked the landing gear on the flatdeck down to the ground and then cranked hard enough to lift at least ten tons off Chrome Stack's chest.

Believe me, Bernice, that's impossible! Number one, those legs aren't designed for that kind of lift, and something should have snapped. Number two, the biggest, strongest skinner you ever meet will say no way, Norman.

At any rate, up she comes—lines disconnected—and Jack pulls slowly away from the trailer and that stupid pipe. Other than a few scratches and a bad case of the shakes, Chrome Stack was fine. Just to slip in the "miracle" bit, Jack admitted later he had no idea how he made a split-second decision to crank the legs, or how he was able to manage something he had never done before or since.

Spooky, huh?

I saved the best one for last. Old "Wheeler" Wally was westbound through Manning Park in southwest BC real early one morning, heading into Vancouver with an empty flatdeck. He had unloaded back at one of the mines in the Kootenays and was now winding his way west along Highway 3, a road that has more twists in it than a used car salesman's contract.

According to Wheeler, the traffic had been scarce in both directions, and a tour bus following well behind was the only company he had, considering he was running solo this trip.

He was already thinking of a pit stop at the town of Hope, about fifteen or twenty miles ahead when a few rocks rolled onto the highway a short way in front of him. Normally, rocks on the road in the mountains are as common as seniors driving slow in the fast lane, but not in this particular spot.

Wheeler couldn't explain it, but something told him to stop. He climbed out of the cab and looked around until the bus running behind caught up to him and stopped as well. Wheeler walked back to the bus, told the driver he felt there was something haywire up ahead and that they had better turn around and go back.

With the rocks on the road ahead and a faint rumbling sound in the distance, the bus driver agreed. He spun around and split. Wheeler, on the other hand, had a forty-five-foot trailer to contend with, and had to back up almost a mile, looking for a wide spot to turn it.

All of a sudden, there was an ear-splitting roar. Clouds of choking dust and rock flew everywhere. Because it was still early morning—pitch black and that dust reducing visibility to near-nothing, even in his headlights—Wheeler had no way of knowing what had happened.

When the dust settled a bit, he found himself staring at a pile of house-sized rocks lying across the highway over 100 feet high, exactly where he and the bus had first stopped.

Only after the authorities had surveyed the damage hours later did Wheeler and everyone else discover that at least a third of Johnson Peak had calved like an iceberg off a glacier, falling across and filling the valley—some 280 feet high and almost 2 miles long.

We aren't just talking a rock slide, boys. The whole face of the mountain broke off and fell over. If Wheeler and the bus had kept going, they would have been right in the middle of the famous Hope Slide.

Creepy, huh? So help me, she's a true story, gang, and according to the history books, it still stands as one of the biggest slides in Canada. There was no way Highway 3 could be dug out, so a new road was laid right overtop that mess.

If you ever get the chance, go take a peek at it.

That Wheeler survived it is pea-pickin' miracle!

PICTURE THIS!

BOYS, I THINK WE HAVE AN IMAGE PROBLEM. John Q. Public has formed a half-dozen pictures of us, and they ain't all good. I've always thought of myself and my fellow diesel demons as pretty professional people, all in all. Of course, I picture us all as clean-cut, alert, courteous dudes with golden haloes above our truckers' hats and feathered wings on our backs, covered by our spotless T-shirts. I imagine a few of us fall a shade short of this, but whoever heard of 100 per cent perfect?

I tell you true, there were enough pictures painted of me to fill an album. There was sure as hell nothing special about little old me, so I assume it happens to all of us. Take your average boss or operations guys. They picture us to be part of the machine. If anything goes wrong, we automatically caused it, being the weakest piece in the rig. I'm pretty sure that's where the term "wing nut" came from. They picture us with a unit number stencilled on our foreheads.

Now, the mechanics picture us with our caps on backwards and both our feet jamming the fuel pedal to the floor while the engine is only turning eight hundred revs and making weird hammering sounds. Naturally, we all know better than that, but the knuckle-skinners invented the term "driver abuse." Mind you, without those guys we'd be unemployed, so I'd better move on.

But first a little story that's kinda typical.

On the way into Vancouver, I develop a glitch with one of those computer-controlled plumber's nightmares, a common brand that's usually dependable. Stupid thing just quit and a bunch of indicator lights came on. Fuel level and plugged filters—those I know about. Everything else under the hood is Latin to me. I get to a phone, call the dealer and tell the shop foreman the rig just quit. I get the usual question.

"What's wrong with it?"

Now how the hell am I supposed to know? I explain the best I can.

"One of the yellow indicator lights has a picture of a small engine with a penis stuck through it. I think the engine may be screwed."

Well, I'm laughing like a lottery winner, but from him, not a toot. Guess he'd heard that one before.

The next picture coming to mind is the one the shippers paint. I'm sure they see us wild-eyed and hyped up, with flying goggles and a rig that will do two hundred miles an hour without stopping or shmucking into something. How many times have you heard them tell you it's a rush load?

Usually after it's taken five hours to stuff it into your trailer. Here's how the conversation goes.

"This load is real 'panic.' It's got to be in Regina (or wherever) by tomorrow night!"

"Well, I'll give 'er my best shot."

I don't want to bore him with details, like I'd have to average one hundred MPH. With the truck and the laws geared to sixty MPH, his "panic load" has as much chance of getting through as a drill bit through a boulder.

I just loved the shipper who told me to "pull the rag" with his Calgary-bound load I'd picked up in Vancouver. It's the middle of winter, and a snow storm has blocked all the main highway passes. When I mention this piddly detail to Speedy Gonzales, he says, "I should have hired my regular carrier."

I lose it and growl out, "Buddy, we all use the same friggin' road. Unless your regular carrier is Air Canada, this freight will be late!"

Well, sure as garlic gives you gas, I hit closed roads and arrive at the Receiver a full day late. I'm expecting another screaming match, but lo and behold, this guy says, "Rush? What rush? I heard about the rotten road conditions, and I'm satisfied you got here in one piece."

Go figure. Two different pictures in one trip.

I admit that episodes like that one are a dime a dozen for all of us, but we all have at least one fracas that paints us pure white on pure black. The blackest one I can remember involved a senior citizen who believed the only good trucker was a dead trucker. I had arrived at a point in my life when I was too sick and stupid to drive, which made me management material. I was now Safety Supervisor in Vancouver for the same outfit I had spent a large chunk of my life driving for.

One hot, summer afternoon, I get a phone call from one of our owner-ops, reporting he'd just had a fender bender. Now this surprised me because he had a driving record like Mother Theresa and the same kind of attitude. He sounded pretty shook up, so expecting the worst, I asked how many were hurt.

"None," he answered. "It's a piddly little bender, but the old boy involved is going ballistic. I'm only a block down the street from you. Can you whip over and calm this old geezer down?"

I arrive minutes later and recognize the usual right-turn, curb-squeezer accident. The rig and fifty-three-foot hi-cube box are halfway around the corner with all the right signals flashing and a four-door import parked beside, with a front bumper shining up at me from the road.

Now, in the great scheme of things, some black tire marks on the door and front fender, plus a missing bumper (and the parts attached to same), do not make a disaster. Unfortunately, that's not the way the motorist saw it. A gentleman somewhere between 80 and 150 years old comes charging up to me with his arms flailing the air. He's the colour of a raw T-bone and hotter than rubber underwear.

"You're going to pay for this! Look what that stupid truck did to my new car!"

"Wait a minute! You mean there's a third vehicle involved? This car has to be two or three years old."

Oh, jeez, wrong thing to say.

"It's new for me, Sonny, and you're going to fix it right now."

This is starting to try my patience just a bit, so I walk over to a grey-haired lady standing calmly on the boulevard.

"Percy will calm down soon," she says. "This is the only new car he ever owned, so he doesn't like to think it's getting on. I told him not to pull alongside your truck because we could see his signal lights, but he gets so impatient. At least nobody was hurt."

Ha! At least one of them was sane. The company and the owner-operator were off the hook and since BC has no-fault insurance, the car could be repaired in a jiffy.

I glance back at the car and notice a little dog with his nose pressed against the glass and his tongue hanging out. All the windows are rolled up and I bet it's 120 degrees in that bomb. I turn to old Percy and tell him he'd better let the dog out before it fries.

"Oh, God! We forgot about Petunia (or whatever the name was)."

But when he yanks the door handle, panic sets in again. The car is all locked up, with the keys in the ignition.

Oh, lovely. First he blames us for demolishing his pride and joy, and now he'll accuse us of murdering his pooch.

"Break a window!" he hollers.

"Relax!" I squeak out. "Did you buy this car from so-and-so up the road?"

Bingo. I get on the owner-operator's cell phone, get the dealer's number from Information and quickly explain the emergency to the salesman who answered. This guy shows up five minutes later with some kind of universal key and frees the mutt. I get the reports filled out, explain to Percy and the Missus how to proceed with repairs and send the undamaged owner-op on his way. Now Percy will love me, right?

Not a chance. His parting words are as follows.

"They shouldn't allow vehicles that size on our roads! You'll hear from my lawyer!"

Oh, well, you can't win 'em all. I still think we're all white knights, but in the immortal words of my old man, "I warned you, smart ass! You should have been a doctor!"

PART FIVE

TERROR AND OTHER
DAILY TRIVIA

WATCH YOUR WEIGHT

TODAY'S TOPIC IS WEIGHT. NO, NO, RELAX. WE'RE talking about the weight of the whole rig, not the pastry craving you gear jammers sometimes get.

Gross weight is one of the major things that truckers face every day, and the ins and outs must be learned the same as swearing or controlling your bladder (when you're paid by the mile you can't be stopping every two hours to tinkle, right, guys?)

What you've got here is a bowling lane, minus the gutters, with eight wheels under the back end and eight wheels under the front end. We won't worry about the two wheels up front for now—the ones that steer.

We call this whole bowling lane thing a "deck." If you put a tin building over it, we call it a van. You can stuff more wheels under all this or make your bowling lane a step deck or a "possum belly," but I'm keeping it simple so your Aunt Isabelle will understand.

Now, these trucks and trailers can carry a whole lot more weight than they usually load on, but the governments who own the roads determine how much bashing their highways will handle. So they make laws. With every province having its own rules, the regulations we have to follow would fill a phone book. A lot of them make sense, but you can sure tell when a particular area's road engineer happens to be the mayor's brother-in-law.

So what's the problem? Just load less, right?

Well, in some cases. If you're hauling ping pong balls or potato chips, you can stuff them to the roof, but steel things and other stuff will stack high enough to split your bowling lane. Fact of the matter is, we get paid by the pound in most cases, so the trick is to get as much on as possible without exceeding the law. Most truckers cut her so close that if a seagull lands on their wagons, they'd probably be over.

Not only do we have to worry about the gross weight of the whole shooting match, but each end can only weigh so much. Now you're into balances and calculations which don't get taught at Gear Cruncher U. Experience and gut feeling are pretty well what we go on.

Governments keep us honest by building little outhouses with long platforms in front of them. These are called "scales," and they're located on the outskirts of most cities and towns. They weigh the whole truck, and if you've put too much freight on it, you have to go into the outhouse and give them some of your money.

Sometimes, if the nice man in the outhouse is seriously

constipated or has fought with his wife before coming to work, he'll come out and inspect your rig. He has tons of laws for tying down loads and maintaining brakes, lights, and other stuff. If he finds anything wrong, you have to go back into the outhouse and give him the rest of your money.

One case like this still sticks in my mind after a whole bunch of years. I get weighed in Moose Jaw, Saskatchewan. The red light comes on at the post in front of me, which tells me I have to go into the outhouse. I've already been weighed three other times on this trip, so I can't be overloaded. I walk in with my fist full of paper, and this cranky old geezer, who'd obviously gone to the Adolph Hitler Scale School, starts yakking at me.

"You're overloaded," he says.

I humbly tell him I can't be, but he swaggers to his phone.

"Tell it to the judge," he says, making a call.

Now, I figure Moose Jaw must be desperate for money, because back then the judge—who was probably the Nazi's cousin—would drive to the scale and rule on the case right there. While I'm standing there wondering what I can say in my defence, his honour shows up just as a rig with a load of new cars pulls onto the scale.

Good grief! The Commandant flashes him the red light too! There's no way in hell this guy can be overloaded. You can't stuff enough cars onto a truck to do it. So in comes the irate driver, and he gets the only words the old coot seems to know.

"You're overloaded!"

"Can't be!"

"Tell it to the judge!"

Boy, this driver is hotter than a Sumo wrestler's jock strap, and as soon as the "judge" walked in, the driver came out with a crack I've never forgotten.

"Judge," he says, "if this world ever needs an enema, this is where they'll stick the tube."

This used car salesman–judge looks at me, cowering in the corner.

"Case dismissed," he says about my little problem, then looks at my red-faced, ranting counterpart.

"Contempt of court!" he hollers. "Three hundred dollars or thirty days!"

Man, I was outta that shack like a ball from a buffalo gun and never looked back.

I figure our biggest problem with weight was a shipper's mistake or, in some cases, downright dishonesty. Nowadays, with the invention of air-bag suspensions and easily-mounted pressure scales on each group of wheels, the guesswork is gone, but that's a luxury we didn't have back then. Unless you suspected there was a problem and weighed on a private scale somewhere, you usually found out you were heavy when you arrived at the People's Outhouse.

Sometimes if you weighed heavy and the shipper's manifest stated a whole lot less, you might get off the hook. If the scale guy just found out his girlfriend wasn't pregnant or something, he would take pity and sell you a permit. I ran into all sorts of scale folks like this, but there was the odd one who trained with the guy from Moose Jaw.

That reminds me of another character who made life tough at the scales. I was hauling logs into Quesnel, BC, and there was a government scale smack dab in the middle of town. For you unfortunates who decided not to truck for a living, I must explain that they don't use bowling lanes for logging. You pull a pole trailer instead, which is eight wheels with a curb-sized steel beam across them and folding steel uprights, eight feet high, hinged on the ends. A skinny piece of pipe called a pole, about thirty feet long, ties these wheels to the back of the truck. There's another "curby" contraption mounted on the truck where the fifth wheel should be, over-top the eight wheels in front. The wagon doesn't need a floor because the logs are as stiff as a new groom, so you only have to support the ends.

Anyway, back to the story. A new scale man arrives in Quesnel with a hatred for all truckers. He stands about six foot three, weighs about 120 pounds and has abnormally big feet. Someone says he looks like a hockey stick, and a nick-name was born.

As Hockey Stick's predecessors were aware, loading logs out in the boonies was a crapshoot. Sometimes the logs would stack a little tighter and you'd end up a shade heavy. With hundreds of us crossing that scale every day, they didn't have the time to mess with minor stuff, so they'd laugh off a few pounds.

Not Hockey Stick. He'd have blocks-long lines of trucks waiting to scale as he wrote up tickets for everything. Every driver cut back his load, also cutting back revenue, to try to please the dork, but a few guys that Hockey Stick was laying for got hassled anyway.

One of these truckers reached his limit, and when he

was told yet again that he was overweight, he lost it.

"How much weight do I have to lose?" he asks.

"Four thousand pounds," Crap-for-Brains replies. "You don't leave the scale until it's corrected."

Oopsy!

Hockey Stick figured that Morris would call the mill and get a machine to come down. Nope.

I forgot to mention that we unload these logs just by tipping traps on the uprights. The front and back uprights collapse on the far side, away from the driver, and that, fellow demons, is just what old Mo did.

Half of Mo's load rumbled over the outhouse just as Hockey Stick leaped out the door.

Morris walks over and grabs the twit by his government-issue jacket.

"Whaddya think? Will that be enough off?"

The news spread like wildfire over a zillion two-way radios, and in an hour over 150 log trucks, empty or loaded, clogged the highway around the scale, on strike until that civil servant was railed out of town.

I figure they must have had a list of complaints a foot-thick on The Stick because when the brass showed up shortly, they herded him into a car and split. There was never any charge laid on our hero, Morris, and a prince of a guy came to run the rebuilt scale. We never saw Hockey Stick again, but the rumour was that he was weighing dog sleds at the Territories border.

Well, I gotta run. The scale ahead is closed, and this load is a little iffy.

BLIND FAITH

WILL SOMEBODY PLEASE EXPLAIN TO ME WHY we have unquestioning trust in people with authority? We pick a perfect stranger, stick him in a position of power, give him or her most of our money and let him run our lives.

"I'm sure they're honest," you'll hear friends say. "I trust them."

You see? Blind faith. Of course, every once in a while one of them gets caught sending Aunt Bernice and her whole family to Bermuda with public funds, but does this shake our trust in the system? Nah.

Anyone with a white smock gets our undivided loyalty. When's the last time you ever doubted a nurse, doctor, dentist, shrink, vet or the corner butcher? We take their word as gospel.

"This won't hurt a bit!" they say, so you willingly stick out your arm, open your big trap wide, hold your dog down or whatever, and then you discover they lied to you. Does this shake our faith in them? Nope—blind faith.

I believe the whole thing started when we were all just rug rats. My folks told me to eat all my veggies so I would grow up big and strong. I ended up five-foot, seven inches tall, and I'm so light I can't go out in a strong wind.

"Let your Aunt Isabel give you a kiss! She loves you."

Truth was, the old bat scared hell out of me. All that was missing was a pointed hat. She gave me little dolls at Christmas until I was fifteen years old. Silly old twit didn't even remember I was a boy!

"Be nice to your grampa. He'll remember you when he passes on."

Hah! Not one thin dime. But truth be told, I didn't mind that one. I loved the old coot anyway.

I tell you, my fellow mileage merchants, this same trust is rampant in our industry. How many times have you heard, "Oh, I'm sure you can get there in time." Or, "That funny clunking sound is your imagination. Keep going." Or, "Go ahead. The storm will blow over." You guessed it. We follow their advice and there we are, way behind schedule because the rig quits in a snow storm.

Of all the times I got bamboozled by that streak of trust, one case stands out like a cockroach on a coffee shop counter. I was driving for an Edmonton-based, flatdeck-heavy-haul-you-name-it trucking company, and I must admit it was mostly a ball. They owned every kind of truck imaginable, and it was chock full of experienced managers and crew. It was truckers' heaven to me.

Anyway, I get called into the "hole" one day (actually, it was the company owner's office. It got the title because the only time a driver got invited in was when something rotten had happened or was about to). The Grand Poobah speaks without looking up from a bunch of drawings on his old desk.

"I got a little job for ya. I don't want to use a kid on this, but you're all I've got for now."

Always with the compliments. He sure knew how to make a guy feel good. He points to one of the drawings and tells me there are a bunch of 125-foot steel beams to move from a fab shop in town to a bridge site seventy-five miles out. About half the route was over country back roads with lots of corners, so the only way to manoeuver was to use two trucks, one on each end. That meant one of the trucks had to back up the whole trip. A whole new learning curve.

A quick peek at the plans told me this was not going to be any romp through the roses.

"What about this height?" I ask. "A seventeen-footer will snag the trolley lines on the main drag through town."

"The wires are eighteen feet high," he replies.

No problem! I convince myself he has to be right because he's the boss, and I'm just brimming with that blind trust again.

We're away with our first load a few days later and things are looking finer than my first girlfriend. I get to drive the lead truck, which happens to be a real ugly but very strong, oversized "J" model Mack. Duke, the guy backing up at the rear—with me pulling both him and the steel beam— is operating like he's done it all his life.

We're under the first set of trolley wires and clearing them by a foot.

See? You just gotta have that trust!

Oops—spoke too soon. Ten minutes up the street we cross an intersection where trolley lines from four different directions meet. Friend, you haven't lived until you hear high voltage lines short out. The crackling sounded like gunfire and pedestrians were scattering like leaves off your lawn.

Duke and I weren't born last Tuesday. We knew that stepping out of those trucks would get us fried, so I inched us through the intersection until the low wires fell off the top of the beam on Duke's end. I flashed my permit at the small army of policemen who arrived, and with no broken wires or damage done, we were gone again.

We wiggle and diddle our way to the bridge site and discover problem number two hundred. The crane to lift this beam off is on the far side of the river! Minutes later, a half-ton shows up and the construction foreman driving it jumps out.

"No, there's no mistake," he says. "You're going to cross the river on the ice bridge. Just stay between those markers."

Oh brother! This was really going to call for blind faith. Granted, it was only mid-March, so the river was still frozen, and the part they had been flooding to create the ice bridge looked solid enough. But there was darn near a foot of melting runoff flowing in places.

Duke looked at that four hundred-foot wide river.

"Don't stop," he said. "No matter what. Even if we break through the ice, the river shouldn't be very deep."

Sheesh. Now I knew Duke was nervous because that was the most words I'd ever heard him string together. Mostly you couldn't get him to say "boo."

We crept in and once the whole shebang was on the ice, you could hear cracking all over the place. You could also see water gushing out of cracks and drill holes a short way upriver. Talk about unnerving!

Looking back and seeing Duke standing on the running board, steering with the door open, was the only real sign of potential doom. Inasmuch as we couldn't see the ice bridge, it was holding and we arrived under the crane alive and dry. As a matter of fact, that invisible bridge held through sixteen loads and only the last two were nail biters.

I must admit that having blind faith in the boss and the contractor worked that time, but it changed my outlook. When somebody walks up to me now and says "trust me," I just grin and roar away.

FEAR NOT!

ONE OF MY YOUNG RELATIVES ASKED ME RECENTLY if I'd ever been nervous driving big rig trucks. This guy is in his early twenties, and I know he's seriously considering truck driving as a career, so I sure don't want to spook him. After some quick thought, I answered.

"Well, trucking is mostly routine, but the unexpected crops up from time to time. Most truckers discover pretty quickly what their rig is capable of and gain a sense of trouble ahead of time so they don't push their luck."

It must have been the answer he was looking for.

"All right," he said cheerily, "I'm going to give it a try."

What I didn't tell him was that truckers are famous for scaring hell out of themselves and sometimes out of other drivers. Road conditions, mechanical failures or unexpected load problems can cause some real butt squeezers. Stands to reason that when you're hurling down the road weighing forty tons or more and something goes haywire, it could get colourful.

What I didn't tell him is that these periods of panic happen to million-milers as well as the newbies. I suppose over-confidence causes a few hectic moments now and then, but mostly it's the unexpected we get blessed with.

I didn't tell him about the first time I saw a real veteran skinner scare the bejeezus out of himself. I was a pimple-faced kid on my first trucking job in the Alberta oil-patch. One of my idols was a senior driver on one of the monster off-road bed trucks. I figured he was totally fearless. His nick-name—"Klink Klank"—was printed in big letters on his shiny, tin hard hat (remember those?), and he looked as tough as the conditions we worked in. I think he got his nick-name because his last name was Klunk. It got lots of laughs, but he didn't seem to mind.

Anyway, the drilling rig a bunch of us had been sent to move was at the bottom of a steep hill. Klink Klank, who was lead truck in our convoy, stops at the brink of the hill, which is obviously a skating rink. Usual procedure would have the bulldozer go down the hill first and chew up the ice a smidge before the trucks attempted it, but the dozer hadn't arrived yet.

Klink the Fearless, who had his tires all chained up, same as the rest of us, volunteered to creep down and scratch up the hill. The truck push and other old hands pointed out that if Klink couldn't stop, his only choice would be to bash into that mountain of steel at the bottom or nose into the sump (a basement-sized hole bulldozed beside the rig to contain the used drilling mud and stuff that came out of the oil well. It forms a small lake).

About halfway down, things turned bad for poor old Klink and he turned into a twenty-five-ton toboggan. With a mighty splash he nosed into the sump, burying the cab in that loon-poop, halfway up his hood. The rig hands got there seconds after and saw Klink was unhurt, but he just sat there, staring out the windshield, still gripping the wheel. Minutes later, the dozer showed up and winched him out, but K.K. never made a move until he was back on dry land. You can bet next month's mortgage payment he scared himself, all right.

I didn't tell my young friend about some of the self-inflicted fear I experienced hauling logs in the BC Interior. Talk about pushing trucks to the limit! Flying down a bull-dozed trail—mistakenly called a road—fully loaded, top-heavy, plowing fresh snow without a hope of stopping if it became necessary—that kind of thing had to make one nervous. The fact that the log bunk on the tractor and the pole trailer behind were designed to part company with the truck if things got out of control was little comfort. If you think about it, the reason they're built like that is because you're expected to spill once in awhile. Mrs. Luck was sure keeping an eye on me as I only tipped two loads through all the years I trucked those pecker poles.

The first one happened in the spring, just before we were to shut down for the thaw. The shoulder of that narrow road gave way, the rig and the load leaned way over. Then the logs were gone like ten bucks on the bar room table. Luckily, the rigging worked like it was supposed to, so my truck stayed upright, but I don't mind telling you, it scared hell out of me.

The second time it happened, I just sort of stepped out

and let her go, but that's a story I'll lay on you another time.

I also neglected to tell my curious young buddy about all the heart-pounders I treated myself to, hi-miling through western Canada. The summer months are pretty routine, all in all, with the tourist traffic posing the only danger. It's the winter time that we earn our money. The prairies, where the wind shines up the packed snow on the roads or in the mountains, where massive snowfalls cause all sorts of problems, are something we face for months on end. Good old Canadian winters! I lost count of the times snow storms or icy hills made me wish I'd stayed in school. I swear, there's no worse feeling in the world than touching the brakes on an icy downgrade and watching your own trailer try to pass you.

And I most certainly didn't tell the young buck about what I figured was my scariest experience. I was westbound through the Fraser Canyon on my way to Vancouver in the middle of the winter. Actually, the run out of Calgary had gone pretty well. I'd only had to chain up once in the Rogers Pass, which was about par for the course at that time of the year. The closer I got to the coast, the better the road conditions got, with less snow and warmer temperatures. If all went well, I figured I'd be in Vancouver in about four hours.

I started down one of the last long, steep hills I had to face, and with the road black as a mechanic's fingernails, I decided I could make up a little time. I'm about halfway down that four-mile grade, going pretty well flat out, near the spot where it's time to start slowing down for a forty MPH curve that I know is at the bottom.

I squish the brake pedal a mite and all hell cuts loose. The trailer gets a mind of its own and the tractor doesn't want to go where I want it to go. I quickly get everything back in a straight line, but I'm doomed anyway. I'm flying on black ice toward a curve I can't possibly make, and below the curve, about two hundred feet down, is the mighty Fraser River. I start thinking about what I'll say to Saint Peter when way down at that curve ahead, lights and yellow flashers start up the hill.

Seconds later, those lights are in my lane, coming right at me. I remember thinking, "Ah, great! I'll die in a wreck rather than in that cold river." Seconds before the head-on, those lights moved over to the other lane. As we flashed past each other, my headlights lit up a government sand truck.

The road ahead of me looked like a beach!

I stomped the brakes as hard as I dared and moaned into that curve just slow enough to drift around it. I was shaking like a duck trying to lay a square egg, so I pulled into a coffee shop in Boston Bar a few minutes up the road to calm down. There was another sand truck parked in the lot, and I found the driver inside. I explained how his partner had realized I was in trouble and had crossed over to my lane to lay that lifesaving sand.

"Thank the guy from the bottom of my hammering heart, please," I says.

"Buddy, you got high-placed friends," the guy replies. "Bert was going to stop here with me but decided to go lose the rest of his load on that hill before he ate!"

Who says truckers don't have guardian angels?

Oops! I just remembered—my young buddy reads all my stories. Relax, youngster. I lived through it, didn't I?

THE HARD PART

WHEN SOMEONE MENTIONS BIG RIG TRUCKING, the first thought is open road, probably in the middle of nowhere, with a chrome-dripping eighteen-wheeler flying flat out. It'd be great if trucking were always like that, but—unfortunately, no way, José!

Granted, we get a little of that luxury on practically every run, but you can count on Mother Nature or your fellow man to throw a screw or two into every trip. But when you have a third thought about it, you remember what the worst part really is.

For me, at least, it was the fact that most freight gets picked up or dropped off in a big city. That made the first and last twenty miles the toughest by far. Some cities are better than others, but none of them is laid out to handle our asphalt battleships.

I'm the first guy to admit that a lot of cities and shippers go the distance to accommodate us. Industrial parks on the outskirts, bypass roads around city centres, and truck terminals near freeways are huge helps. It's when we have to venture into the bowels of these cities with our bedroom blocking the rear view that we really start to earn our money.

My cap is off to the drivers who pull trailers around these cities for a living. The only advantage most of them have is that they manoeuver around familiar territory and they aren't saddled with the bunk. Matter of fact, I did a few years of toot-around-town stuff myself in Vancouver, and I tell you true, there's never a dull moment. There are just some places a fifty-three-foot trailer behind a 245-inch wheelbase Kenworth shouldn't go.

Let's face it, most Canadian cities were being built when trucks were chain-driven and nobody would have dreamed how big and heavy these pavement pounders would get. As we're all painfully aware, most cities offer narrow streets with bumper-to-bumper traffic, tight corners, and tunnels or underpasses that looked real roomy in 1920.

Okay. So here comes Larry Lease Operator in his long-nose Pete, tooling along in the centre of three lanes of traffic that stretches to the horizon. On both sides, cars are clearing him—and one another—by inches. It's pouring rain; he's got to turn right pretty soon, he figures, and there's an underpass coming up that sure as hell looks low enough to peel the ceiling off his fifty-three-foot Great Dane. The city map is spread open on the jump seat, but the last chance he had to glance down, it was more confusing than a loan application. You can bet your Tony Lamas that he's sweating a bit.

Oh, Mother! I can sure remember a couple of those first-time-in-town nightmares. The one that stands out like a live mouse at a quilting bee is my virgin trip into Regina, Saskatchewan. Actually, I caused myself a lot of trouble because I didn't follow orders. I was team driving a fully-loaded cabover Kenworth from Vancouver with Sparky, an old hand, a great guy, and a big time practical joker. He'd half-assed told me how to get to our destination while he climbed into the bunk a few hours short of Regina. His last words were "Wake me up at the city limits."

Well, as I approached the outskirts with Sparky sound asleep, it occurred to me that he'd appreciate a little extra sack time, and I figured I could find my own way. What the heck! I was a prairie city boy and a fearless hi-miler.

But twenty minutes into the city and I knew I'd screwed up. Every vehicle in Saskatchewan was on the same street I was on. I'd just gone through an intersection where I was supposed to turn, and ahead of me, the terrain sure looked like downtown. I'm now stopped and stuck in a traffic jam with an RCMP car right in front of me.

You're right, it was time to wake up Sparky. Wouldn't you know, he was one step ahead of me. He'd already peeked out the curtain, figured out what I'd done, and his twisted mind had figured out a way to rub my nose in it. Mr. Practical Joker had straightened out a coat hanger, slipped it over the curtain rail, and snagged the air horn chain that was dangling out of the headliner. Then he'd yanked it back and bent the hanger over the curtain rod. That pair of seven-mile air horns sounded like the Queen

Mary docking, and in the seconds it took for my heart to drop out of my throat and back into my chest, I figured out what that warped twit had done.

While I'm trying to remove that hanger, and with Sparky splitting a gut behind me, I notice the cop get out of his car and slowly walk back to my door. The most patient policeman I have ever met looks up at me.

"You can turn off the horn now," he says politely. "It won't help."

I tell him I'm desperately trying to stop it, but the mental patient I'm transporting isn't being much help. I finally wrestle the horn free, but my noise is replaced by car horns, alerting the cop and me that the traffic has moved ahead. The officer looks up one more time, mutters, "Have a good day" or "Goddamn truck drivers"—I'm not sure which—then heads back to his car. Imagine, no bullet through my horn and no ticket! I suspect he had to deal with practical jokers too. Anyway, Old Stupid got out of the bunk and put us back on the straight and narrow.

The other strange-city driving episode still makes me stare into space and shake my head when I think of it. This little beauty happened to me in Vancouver, which just happens to be the broken drive shaft capital of Canada. Stands to reason, as the city is smack dab in the middle of the mountains, with one side of it at sea level. The only way in or out of the city is up or down.

Some of the hills in this town would bring tears to a mountain goat. Even the truck routes through the city have some grades that could stall a bulldozer. You can pick out the old-timers on some of these climbs because they're taking it slow. These hills are scarred up with gouges from breaking drive lines or pieces of trannies from the guys in a rush who tried to grab a faster gear. I crap you not—a couple of them are mine.

Babble, babble, back to the story.

My first few trips into Vancouver from small-and-flat Edmonton were a piece of cake, with trailer switches at the terminal near the freeway and a couple of voyages into the city following another truck, which knew where it was going. Or even having a team driver with me who could navigate. One trip, however, I arrive with an empty flatdeck at our terminal, late at night, and find written orders to load downtown first thing in the morning.

Oh, rats! I'd never heard of Granville Island, in the centre of the city, but I had my trusty map, so what the heck. The truck route map on the wall at the terminal looked all wiggly to where I was going, and I could see a lot faster route on my map. I figured that even if I went off a truck route, the police would be prowling for burglars, not empty trucks.

I head right out, using my route, and figuring on a little sleep at the shipper's gate. I plan to go straight west on Broadway and eventually onto one of the side streets, hooking up from there to the road onto Granville Island. Through the usual rain, I pick a likely side street and start dropping. No problems until I realize that my headlights aren't aimed at the road any more. I break over the crest of a block-long hill, which appears to go straight down, with a dead end at the road I need to turn onto! I stamp the brake pedal to the floor, which of course, gives my empty flatdeck permission to go its own way. There's no way that wet road was going to let me stop before I flew into the intersection and either smucked an unsuspecting car or crashed into a ground floor apartment in the building ahead of me.

Well, the patron saint of gear grinders came through. There wasn't another vehicle in sight, and the curb on the far side brought me to a stop, with the steering wheels up on the sidewalk. When I willed myself to breathe again and took stock of both myself and the rig, all appeared to be in order. I quick-like-a-bunny backed my Kenworth off the sidewalk and was gone like a cheap toupee in a tornado.

No sleep for me at the shipper's gate, for sure! I just sat there, swearing I'd never leave another truck route and just itching to get out of town and hit the open road, where this metal motel truly belongs.

OLD COOTS CONFERENCE

WHAT A BUMMER! I JUST SUFFERED THROUGH another birthday, and I'm feeling almost prehistoric. It's not like I laboured on the Pyramids or anything, but I'm getting up there. I still take great interest in any classy eighteen-wheelers whizzing by, but I've started noticing how young the skinners all seem to be. Well, that started me thinking of the past, like all old coots tend to do, and how much things have changed in our racket over forty years.

It also occurred to me that there must be scads of wrinkled-up asphaltologists out there doing the same. I figured it would be a riot to gather us all together and swap stories, but who the hell would put up with that many yahoos in one room? I finally decided that a story directed at my old pothole-seeking partners might do the trick and might even give the youngsters a snicker. They may not believe what we had to face, but cross my screwed-up ticker, she's all true.

Okay, all you majorly-mature split-shifters out there, this Bud's for you! Get your nurse to pour you a glass of prune juice, park your walker, ease into a soft chair and turn off your Ferlin Husky tape. We're going back forty years, boys, and I've got no intentions of yapping about power, regulations, or "bigger is better." The basics we tolerated are enough to make anyone cackle.

How about our stump-mounted seats? Remember that small fire hydrant with the steel chair mounted on it? Two or three inches of foam rubber covered with vinyl separated us from the holes, ruts and rocks. It was more like a saddle than a seat. On a rough road, we spent more time hanging from the steering wheel to keep our moneymaker out of that kidney-crusher than we did sitting in it. A lot of us were short and fat, but we didn't start out that way. The constant jarring from that seat settled our bodies like shaking settles wet concrete. As I've mentioned before, you haven't lived until you go into a dip flat out, mounted on one of those monsters, when your bean hits the headliner on the way in and your spine is driven into your skull on the way out. We call that the good old days!

Speaking of sitting in the seat, what about that manual steering? Guiding the rig through city traffic would make an ape sweat. There was no way in hell you could turn the wheel more than a crank or two with the rig parked. I can imagine how funny we must have looked, rocking the rig back and forth to turn the wheel in tight spots. Joe Average must have figured we'd split our crystals and couldn't decide which direction to go.

Matter of fact, that direct steering could be a downright hazard on occasion. What you had there was a roughly two-foot-diameter steering wheel trying to guide two, four-foot-diameter wheels in a direction they preferred not to go. Steering box full of reduction gears or not, if those steering tires hit a rut, a rock or a curb, that tiller would rip out of your hands faster than a business card out of an insurance salesman's shirt.

Sprained thumbs were a trademark in our business, same as missing fingers on a carpenter. You could always tell an experienced driver by the way he gripped the wheel. No way did we wrap our thumbs around the inside, buddy! They were always up top, alongside our fingers, where they were nice and safe.

Speaking of tires, remember the bias rubber with flaps and inner tubes? Driver's nightmare! If the rig was parked in the cold for any length of time, we got eighteen flat spots, all in the same place. So when we started rolling, we had to put up with this humungous clunking and jumping until everything warmed up. We got twice the punishment if we had to hook up to a frozen wagon, so now we had two sets of flat spots in different places. Makes my hips hurt just thinking about it.

The very worst thing about them was when those tires went flat. If the steel stem of that inner tube slipped inside while you were cruising, it would slash the bejeezus out of the tube and the tire, and eventually the whole shootin' match would catch fire. That meant we had to stop every hour or two and thump every tire to check for flats, especially through the mountains, where sharp rocks on the road were a constant headache.

The only thing we could do with a tire fire was cross our fingers and put our boots to the floor. If it was our lucky day, the burning rubber would eventually fling itself off the rim without setting the rest of the tires or the trailer on fire.

Hey, Zorro! Lean in a little! Remember the time you got a flat on that single drop with the donut tires and she started to smoke? By the time you stopped and ran to the back, all eight were in flames. I hadn't seen the boss that mad since he got caught using purple fuel in his Buick.

Cackle, cackle!

Williams exhaust brake. Now, there was a joke. It was supposed to retard the engine, but it didn't even retard the exhaust. Useless as foam rubber crutches. And metal-mounted marker lights! No rubber shock-preventers at all. One decent pothole and half of them went out. We had to carry boxes of bulbs with us to keep the trailers lit up.

I made a big mistake one day on the Vancouver water-front. I was getting my flatdeck trailer loaded by one of the big forklifts and the operator had the nasty habit of approaching the side of the trailer with his fork full of pipe, up high. He'd bump his machine against the trailer as he lined up, then he'd back off to let the pipe roll off the forks. That little bump was enough to blow all the marker lights, so I asked him to take it easy.

"No problem," he says, and comes back minutes later with another forkful. He rams the side of the trailer at full tilt. The deck slides sideways a foot, the pipe dribbles off his forks onto the dock on the far side of the trailer, and I head for high ground.

After the noise and dust settles, the rather large operator steps out of his machine and says, "There! Is that better?" I crap you not. That was the last time I ever told anyone how it should be done.

Hand flog. Admit it, guys—if something could be lifted by hand, that's the way she got stowed. Oh, sure! There were pallets and forklifts around, but I guess the shippers figured we needed exercise, what with all that sitting around we did. Evil swines! Oak kegs to steel pipe, we were pilots, I guess—pick it up here and "pilot" in there.

How often do you hear that the highways are in bad shape these days? When I hear the whining, I usually reply, "You mean that divided six-lane strip of asphalt stretching in a straight line from here to you-name-it?"

Sonny (the guy's in his forties and I call him Sonny. Maybe I *am* getting old!) the only time we got to drive in a straight line was when we didn't make it around the corner and we slid off our one stupid lane. Take this Number 2 from Edmonton to Calgary, for instance. That sucker joined at least eight towns with a two-lane road, and every one of them had a speed limit. That was a six or eight hour trip for us that you can do now in four, or even less if you press the fuel pedal with both feet.

The government was building that six-lane runway alongside the old road in spots back then, and I found myself thinking I should stop and give them a hand to speed things up. When we finally got to use it, even the frost heaves were acceptable.

Heck, that's only an example. All the roads in western Canada were town-joiners to start with. I raise my tumbler of Geritol to the folks who designed and built those nice, wide, town-bypassing launch pads.

Speaking of highway construction, back then the worst nightmare me and the guys faced was the Fraser Canyon section of the Trans Canada in BC They were still boring the tunnels and we had to skirt two or three of them on a single-lane, temporary rock trail, barely glued to the side of the mountain.

We were hundreds of feet above the thundering Fraser River. Rocks would bounce down from above, roll across the road or smuck the truck before disappearing over the cliff. It was more nerve-wracking than a tax audit. If we hit these stretches at night, with the ever-present fog bank obscuring everything, we discovered that we could hold our breath for ten full minutes until we got past.

Another problem was making the road stay where they'd put it. Rock slides would come down and take half-mile sections of the new road out, right down to the Fraser. Me and my partner, Sinful Sid, darn near bought the farm at one of these slides. We were traveling south—oh, wait just a minute.

Hey, Sinful! Wake up! I'm telling about our Canyon scrape.

Anyway, we're on a fairly straight stretch of brand new pavement. I'm driving late one night when old Sid pokes his head out of the curtain to ask me something. I turn my head to yap with him and stop paying attention for way too long. All of a sudden, without a word, Sid's eyes go the size of plates and he disappears into the bunk.

I spin around in time to see a couple of flare pots, a "Slow to 30" sign and then the new, bright-white line disappears about a hundred yards ahead of us. I hit the binders, but not near fast enough, and we fly over the edge of a slide, heading straight for the river. It became obvious that this slide had happened earlier in the day, and the construction guys had run a bulldozer over this mess so that traffic could still move.

With the tractor and trailer wheels all chattering and jumping over this rock-covered series of ripples and potholes, my main concern became negotiating the slight bend at the bottom of this log-chute without the rig chattering itself sideways and dropping us into the drink. The second concern was the freight on our flatdeck shaking loose and slipping into the sleeper with Sinful.

Against my better judgment, I released the brakes, ordered power to the drivers, whipped around the bend and bounced up the other side without fainting. I pulled over, wondering how I'd ever pry my fingers off the steering wheel and looking around to see if Sid was one of the things that had shaken out of the sleeper.

Suddenly, his pure-white face appeared through the curtain.

All he said was, "They gotta make better blinkety-blank signs. It should read, 'BLEEPIN' ROAD GONE. GOOD BLEEPIN' LUCK!' "

Then he disappeared again.

None the worse for wear, we were gone, and I'd better do the same. Sparky's hollering for the bedpan, Little John's last wheeze sounded funny, and he's fighting for air. Besides, Sinful has gone back to sleep, and it's way past my nappy time, too.

Cackle, cackle!

PART SIX

GOOD, BAD,
AND ROTTEN

TIME FLITS AWAY

WOULDN'T IT BE GREAT TO GET YOUR HANDS on the sadistic swine who dreamed up the first tight truckers' schedule? I'll bet you a sheepskin seat cover that the low-life wasn't even a hi-miler. He's probably in Japan trying to get their trains to run faster.

If you could take your present day schedule-setter for a trip and show him how most schedules get shot to pieces— when they get to see snow drifts, rock slides, road-blocking wrecks, bumper-to-bumper Winnebagos testing to see how slow they can go without stalling the engine and a full house at Molly's Meatloaf Emporium with only one waitress on duty—they'll catch on.

The flight plans have gotten so tight that we've become the most important employees in North America. Not only are we given written arrival date and time, there's a tach recording every move we make, satellite tracking to keep an eye on the progress and a phone or computer hook-up in the cab, so they can let us know we're late. Even bleedin' pilots don't rate this much attention!

Just for laughs, I'd love to transfer a satellite gizmo off my truck onto one of those campers at a truck stop one day and picture the brass at our home office go insane as they see the blip stop every twenty minutes so that Percy and Mildred can tinkle. Jeez, it'd be worth the pink slip.

Trucking companies have to take the heat, really. They make delivery promises we can't keep and use names like Quick As Air, Speedy Delivery, and Jet Express, convincing receivers and shippers that overnight service is in the bag. Good grief! Most outfits don't even warehouse the stuff anymore. Our wagons are the warehouses, and we start ducking lead if the load is late. It's only a matter of time until someone forms Speed of Light Truck Lines: "We'll have it there before you place the order!"

In the meantime, we have to run flat out, leaning our hi-cubes over so far in the corners that we get grass stains on the sides while the sign on the van doors reads, "If this truck is speeding, phone blah, blah, blah." Go figure.

Holy herring-choker! That turned into a bit of a rant. Well, ex-ka-USE me! Anyway, the good news is that schedules weren't always this goofy. It's not like we were allowed to wander around the country willy-nilly, wasting money like politicians do, but there was a little give and take.

Not all that long ago, there were no "hours of driving" regulations or log books to contend with, so travel times were a crap shoot. If the weather was good, the traffic was light and Old Fang was shooting fire out of the chrome chimney, you might arrive at your destination hours—or a day, even—early.

The next trip, everything you touch turns to cow frisbees.

On the prairies, it gets colder than a grave digger's shovel, and things break. Rain measured in feet comes down in the BC mountains, washing rocks the size of Hondas onto the highway. There were a million things that could make you wish you had stayed in school. Point is, the company brass, the shippers, and the receivers all knew we had this crud to face and allowed for it.

Strap me to your wagon and stone me if I'm wrong, but I think our running time was not far short of today's screaming million-horsepower road-rippers. Mind you, power played a big part in our travel time too. The older, under-gutted 220 and 250 HP motels would try to keep up with the 335 and 350-equipped rigs coming out. This called for working the bejeezus out of those no-blower six-bangers.

I still limp to this day from trying to push the fuel pedal through the floor for hours on end. Some of the mechanically-minded old hands like Hydraulic Jack loved to mess with the fuel pump buttons on the old 220 squirrel runs and "up" the power or RPMs a bit. Unfortunately, this also increased the heat, which—if ignored—could melt the engine into a solid chunk of steel with a couple of burned belts hanging off it.

The Alberta-based outfit I worked for had one 220-powered Hayes Clipper cabover amongst a whole raft of 250-horse Kenworths. All the greying gear-grinders out there will fondly remember a 1954 model of that brute. The gauges were all in a panel above the driver's head, which made for a stiff neck while keeping an eye on things. The windshield was a huge wrap-around bay window, stretching from the rooftop to the driver's knees and wrapping around to the doors on either side. We're talking fish bowl, gang!

Anyway, this was Hydraulic Jack's rig for a time, and my steed, Old Fang, was a 250 KW. It was rumoured that Jack had monkeyed with his fuel pump and could stay with our new fire-belchers, so on one trip I was happy as a puppy chewing Granddad's slipper when we were in a four company-truck convoy, climbing through Rogers Pass, westbound.

Ladies, anyone will tell you that this BC mountain climb to Nosebleed Summit is miles long and darned steep. This separates the real trucks from the manure-spreaders. At the bottom, Hydraulic Jack was dead last, but three-quarters of the way up, he had sacked Red Wine Robbie, and caught up to Old Fang, leaving Zorro in the lead (as always).

This last climb was the steepest part, taking us through a handful of long tunnels and not levelling off until the summit.

"Hardy, har, har!" I belch. "Jack's chances of sacking me on this grade are goose-egg, because my engine is just hovering on the take-yer-boot-out-of-it point. So his old Unit Two Bits must be ready to perk a pot of tea!"

One more glance in the go-backwards wipes the smirk off my kisser.

"Sparky!" I holler towards the sleeper. "Would you believe Frenchman (Hydraulic Jack) is pulling out to pass us?"

Sparky bails onto the jump seat and we both stare out the driver side window as that old Hayes inches up beside us. We're side-by-side, pulling into one of the longest tunnels, when I notice the muffler and stack on that old truck is a weird colour, and heat is just shimmering off it. All of a sudden, the top of the muffler and the chrome extension just fall over, and there is a tooth-loosening roar filling the tunnel.

Old Fang is contributing a little of the racket, but Old Two Bits has burned the guts out of her muffler and is now shooting smoke and flames through a straight trail to the engine room. The few unfortunate tourists going both directions stopped in their tracks, figuring the tunnel was collapsing or something.

I immediately slacked off and let Hydraulic Jack pass for fear that the old girl was due to explode and "off" us all.

Minutes later, we all pulled over at the summit, expecting to hear Old Two Bits seize up and meet its demise. Granted, it was snapping and crackling like a radiator in a cheap hotel, but that old war horse was idling smooth as a baby's bum.

Sparky couldn't wait to run up to Jack and jazz him about it.

"Oh, man! You had to see it! There were flames a foot high coming out, with pitch-black smoke, and right on top of the flame was this old burning leather boot! You were pressing the pedal so hard that your shoe must have gone through the pump!"

Well, Hydraulic got the last laugh, telling Sparky, "I am beat you good, eh, Spark? Maybe Donny only wear slipper, eh? Got to put boot in." (Jeez, that rotten French-Canadian humour!)

You woulda figured that with all this show of raw power, we would have been way ahead of schedule, but as luck would have it, we blew our lead. All four of us stopped at our favourite Gag and Heave, west of Revelstoke. We were quickly followed by three westbound company rigs, two buddies with Emors Cattle Haulers and a vw van with four women somewhere in the sixteen-to-twenty-year range. Did this have SEMINAR written all over it, or what?

The trucks were all parked and locked. I phoned dispatch with tire problems. Hydraulic reported engine overheating. Red Wine called in with suspected food poisoning, and Zorro claimed "getting funny noise from motor but guy coming for look-see."

Did we make our drops on time? Nah! We were a little late. Did the dispatchers believe all our woes? Probably not, but nothing said.

My goodness! How time flits away!

GOODBYE, BEANS!

OLD DONNY IS PACKIN' GOOD NEWS THIS TIME, my fellow gear-ologists. I do believe these stories I write—about the day-to-day crappola we face—are starting to change the image Mr. and Mrs. Public have of us. The old picture of us standing beside a rig lying on its side across the highway, with freight scattered for a mile, is fading. The new image of us being upstanding, clean-shaven members of this planet, just doing our thankless jobs, has taken root.

I've met a zillion folks since we gave them a peek into our diesel-powered profession, and they're curious as all get-out about the inner workings of our big rigs. I'll bet you a Flying "J" Truck Stop T-shirt that the non-trucking masses are asking you guys all about it too, whenever you're anchored up.

Personally, I get a real kick out of answering their questions, even if some of them are as confusing as a politician's platform. Just recently I'm having lunch with a bevy of angels—my book publisher and her crew, actually—when the questions start to fly.

"How can you remember all these events?" they asked. "What triggers the event into a story? How come you're so handsome?" (I just threw that last bit in.) Then they asked, "What's the worst problem drivers face?"

"Mmmmm, well, eerrrr," I says, trying to look serious and wise, but failing both. "I think the stories come in association with something, really, and come to think of it, just sitting in this restaurant has me thinking of one."

I told it to them, and now I'll tell it to you.

One of the worst problems for long haul truckers—at least it used to be—was food. Oh, sure, there have always been truck stops ("eat-its-and-beat-its" or "gags-and-heaves" to us rubber-mounted warriors), and through the summer months you can usually find one when the growlies set in. Even then it can be a problem, because parking seventy-five feet of snarling steel takes a fair amount of room. Even if there's a "Trucks Only" sign posted, Percy and Emma figure their half-ton Dodge with a tent trailer tied behind qualifies them to screw a ravenous gear-slammer out of a place to land.

Sheesh! How many times have you heard a four-wheeler state, "We always stop where the trucks are, because the food will be good!" Totally wrong, Rennie. We stop where we have room to park. The restaurant could be serving fried seagull, but we make it do.

And I don't like to give away all our trade secrets, but that "Trucker's Breakfast" come-on is a crock of crow cookies.

For guys who sit hour after hour with absolutely no exercise, steak and eggs rumbling around in their guts is about as useful as training wheels on a tractor. Heavens to Mergatroid! Most of our meals are peaches and toast, or a greasy burger if we're in a big hurry.

I'm convinced that one of the great new accessories you can get mounted in your tin steed is a fridge. I'd have given up my Freightliner leather-sleeved jacket for one of those on occasion.

My truck, Old Fang, just barely had room for me, my co-pilot, and what meagre belongings we could store at the end of the sleeper. Any food we took along—some of which was an absolute "must"—had to be strapped in a box on the walking board behind the cab.

Now we all know that Canadian winters are ten months long; then you get two months of bare spots. It was usually colder than your ex-wife's divorce lawyer outside. The food would stay fresh to the point where sliced bread froze hard as a cedar shingle, and canned meat felt like a hand grenade.

Granted, there were truck stops of one description or another spotted along most highways, but (a) we were off-highway a fair amount, and (b) Mrs. Nature could dump multi-feet of snow on the road between you and the next gag-and-heave, so one had to be equipped to survive until the snowplows dug you out.

Making sandwiches was no big deal. The bread thawed out quite nicely in the windshield defrost slots, and you sat on your can of meat until your hemmorhoids screamed.

Then lunch was served. A carton of milk could be torn open and eaten like a popsicle. Nummy!

Hot meals took a little longer, because our stove was the engine exhaust manifold. If your mobile café was a conventional cab with an easy-opening hood, putting on supper was a cinch, but Old Fang was a cabover with the engine tucked underneath. This meant that one had to climb up on the frame behind the cab and reach way in to place the canned delicacy onto the manifold.

My first attempt at this culinary camp-out ended in disaster. While reaching in to place my large can of beans—frozen hard as a brick—I touched a hot hose or something and dropped my main course! Now I had to climb under the rig and fish out that stupid can with my burned hand. Finally, with supper on the manifold and me back in my nice, warm cab, it occurred to me that the genius who had recommended this food preparation technique hadn't mentioned how long a can of beans would take to heat. With my rumbling restaurant safely parked in a pull-off, and the stove set at high idle, all I could do was wait.

Well, fellow campers, it didn't take long at all. About ten minutes into the operation, there's a medium-sized explosion under the cab. Good grief, sounds like a rod going through the side of the block. Hold the phone, Phyllis! Old Fang is still running, so it can't be that. Oh-oh, bad smell. Time to get out, take a peek and retrieve supper.

Friend, I'm here to tell ya, my bean supper was sprayed all over the engine, all over the ground, and what was left of the tin can was embedded in the insulation overtop the engine! I find out days later from that genius that he forgot to tell me to poke a hole in the can before I stuck her on the manifold.

The embarrassing part was that it wasn't possible to wash all that sticky crap off the engine, so for two weeks after the truck smelled like a tanning factory. Live and learn, huh?

The point of all this is that food is one of a trucker's main concerns. Heck, you dump a couple hundred gallons of fuel into your steed, and she'll run around the clock, but the pilot has to fuel up a lot more often than that. I drove in the Alberta oil patch for a bit, and those guys had the solution down to a science. Picture that off in the boonies, there are no truck stops, restaurants, corner stores, or anything. Every oil drilling rig has its own cook shack and eating area capable of feeding its own crew, plus the thirty-odd truck drivers who show up when it's moving time.

Before sun-up on the day of the move, everyone is fed as much as they can hold, and bags of sandwiches are given to everyone to cover lunch. Then the first thing to be loaded onto a truck is that cook shack and the cooks. If the rig is to be moved a long distance, the shack will stop at a six or eight hour drive away and everyone will be fed in the still-trailer-bound shack as they arrive.

Short distance or long, the first thing set up at the new site is the cook shack and the crews' bunkhouses. Okay, now we're talking steak and eggs! Cold weather, insanely hard labour and long hours gave you an appetite the size of a politician's ego!

Ah, jeez! I just remembered the greatest truck stop I

ever grazed in. It was about halfway between Revelstoke and Salmon Arm, slap-dab in the middle of the Rockies. The joint was a real oasis to the double-clutchers running the Trans Canada between Vancouver and the rest of the old Moose and Maple Leaf. When you pulled into their roomy parking area, you had just come through Rogers Pass, or you were headed for it. As I've whined before, that guy, Roger, must have hated truckers. Steep climbs, strong winds, and snowfalls measured in feet made that trail a real cheek-squeezer. That truck stop was the place where we celebrated living through it again or tried to cram down a two-day supply of vittles at one meal, just in case the frequent storms or avalanches stranded us.

The owners of that sweet spot appreciated the hi-milers as much as we did them, and they went out of their way for us. They discouraged tourist traffic by slapping "Truck Parking Only" signs all over the place and "Reserved for Truckers" signs at half the booths in the coffee shop. The mechanical and tire repair shops were staffed around the clock. Brother, that tire shop was a beehive of activity, what with sharp rocks dropping onto the highway steady. You could figure on blowing at least one skin on that stretch, especially with the bias tube-and-flap rubber we ran. The really special thing that those hi-miler heroes did—besides having the waitresses live in the onsite motel—was something you won't believe.

The stupid laws back then had something called The Lord's Day Act, which forced businesses to close and restricted trucking on Sundays. The restaurant had to close, but like the great, old owner said, "There's no law against leaving the door unlocked!" The grill was left on, the fridge was unlocked, and written instructions about how to make coffee in the big urn were taped on it. A big bowl with loose change sat on the counter, with a note stating, "Pay what you think it's worth."

Gang, who would put us on the honour system today? Nada.

Turns out, some truckers are great cooks, including my co-pilot, Nicky the Wop (no offense to the Italian community, but that's what we called him then), who whipped up tubs of spag-and-sauce like a pro.

Pasta Fazoolla! That fridge was stuffed with steaks and you-name-it, and boys, we're talking banquet! Needless to say, we always overpaid, and that bowl of cash would overflow.

Don't that just warm your cockles? (Whatever the hell those are?)

Drive proudly, gang, and don't forget to poke a hole in your lunch.

HEAVY DANGER

"TRUCK DRIVING IS DANGEROUS WORK, AND we deserve better loot!" my double-clutching buddy tells me the other day.

"Ain't it the truth?" I reply. "But I doubt the world puts us in the same heroic class with fire fighters, cops or sales clerks at a ladies' wear sale."

Granted, our job can get a little iffy when the waste hits the agitator, but as long as you keep your 20-20s open, hi-miling is usually pretty routine. Lash me with your CB aerial if you think I'm wrong, but I figure our diesel-powered occupation is a whole lot safer than it used to be.

"Bull tweet!" my eager young gear-slapper says. "We still run the same roads and hills that you fossils did, and the only difference is that you were powered with steam!"

Ooo, that hurt. He's just lucky my arthritis was acting up that day, or I'd have given him some free dental work.

At any rate, I stayed cool.

"Dangerous truckin'? You wanna hear about dangerous truckin'? Watch my lips!"

My very first trucking job would have sent shivers up a commando's spine. I was hired at seventeen to drive a converted dump truck in a steel mill. The old girl was a story-and-a-half, tandem-axle, gas-driven GMC, rigged to haul slag away from the steel furnace. Slag is the waste you get when you melt scrap iron into usable steel.

They pour this molten crud into a slag pot, which looks like half a grapefruit, eight feet across. Then they stick a lifting hook into it and let that cast iron pot cool while they pour the good stuff—the pure steel—into a big-mother ladle. Now they call in Donny, the slag hauler. That twenty-ton, half-ball-shaped chunk of slag is just cool enough to hold its shape while it's lifted out of the pot and very softly placed onto old Unit 2.

We're talking lava with a very thin skin here, and you couldn't get any closer than fifteen feet from it without feeling the burn start. Obviously the truck had to be rigged for this, so it had solid rubber tires that would still burst into flames on occasion but couldn't explode. It also had asbestos wrapping around all the hydraulic rams and hoses, but the oil would still start to boil in less than ten minutes.

The gas tank behind the seat was never more than half full and had to be wrapped in asbestos. The dump bed had low sides, lined with brick, topped with two inches of steel, and two railroad tracks ran parallel, the length of the bed, to keep the slag from rolling around and also to aim it off the back end when it got dumped. A massive asbestos-lined steel shield extended from the front of the box over the cab of the truck.

Seconds after that slag pop landed on the truck, you had to open the door, as the heat was almost unbearable. The tricky part was to haul this thing just under a mile to the slag field without shaking it open. If it split open, and the lava got loose, it would melt anything it touched—truck, Donny and all. Sometimes they would simply explode when they hit wet ground, so you always kept your head down near the seat when you dumped.

Now, do the numbers. Three furnaces, three pots each per shift. This meant nine times a day old Donny could get fricasseed! Was this a Compensation Board nightmare? Was this dangerous? Damn straight.

Well, Pedro, Blackhawk, and I lived through it. Then came the bigger furnaces, eighty-five-ton slag pots and massive machines that could pack pot, slag and all, out to the field with nobody getting anywhere near it. Safety *rules*, man!

The next step up the gear-grinder's ladder was pulling trailers locally—in and around Edmonton in my case. Same old story, as far as safety was concerned. Like most factories, steel mills will roll one particular size of steel bar for days, so they don't have to change rollers. This means that usually, by the time they got around to a certain size, it was in great demand, so it got bundled and boarded onto our trailers straight off the assembly line, with the heat still shimmering off it.

Actually, it was quite a sight to crawl through town with the flatdeck smoking and the steel sizzling like sausages on a spit. The tricky part was standing on top of this smoldering mess to hook up or unhook the chains used to handle the stuff. You haven't lived until the soles of your work boots catch fire and you do a five-minute Highland Fling to put the flames out.

The other real unsafe parts of this circus were the lack of scales and regulations. Those steel reinforcing bars were usually sixty feet long, which called for a forty-foot flatdeck trailer hooked to an under-powered 1 HC or GMC tractor with a single-axle, pole trailer at the back end to carry the extra length.

Did we have lights or brakes on those pole trailers? Naw! That's for sissies. Did we heap on as much steel as we figured we could pull up the hills out of the river valley? Of course! Could we have held her on the hill if the squirrels died or we had to anchor quick? No hope, Harry! Was all this insanely dangerous? Hoo boy!

The final step up to the glorious long haul finally arrived, and we still acted as if we were indestructible. Now we're talking raw power, like 250 horses, and you're right— we were travelling over the same roads you are. Difference was, those highways were still being built. We were hauling the steel into Rogers Pass to build the snow sheds.

We were also hauling the bridge-building stuff up the Yellowhead. There were twenty-something single-lane, Bailey bridges we had to cross back then. They were still blasting the tunnels in the Fraser Canyon, so we had to skirt those sections clinging to the edge of the mountain on our way to and from the coast. Maxi-brakes weren't available yet, so if we broke an airline, it was goodbye brakes. Worse yet, retarders or "jake brakes" were an option that our company figured we didn't need. Scales were few-and-far-between, so a little extra weight was normal.

Was all of this dangerous? You can bet your eagle-feathered stetson it was. You don't need me to tell you that things are 100 per cent different now. You've got double the power, double-width roads, scales every two blocks and enough regulations to fill a phone book.

I just said "different," not better! I suppose if the fuse blows on your retarder, if your computerized engine acts up, or if you lose the satellite signal and the freeway is backed up, you could be facing a little danger, right?

Tell you true, I've had closer calls on passenger airplanes than I can remember in the rigs.

One trip, I'm flying from Hawaii to Vancouver on a chartered United Airline DC-8. That tin crow had already departed ten hours late because one of its four jet engines was screwed up and had to be replaced. We're finally in the air by a couple of hours when the pilot comes on the intercom to fill us in on a small problem.

"The plane has lost all hydraulic pressure, which operates everything on this crate," he says, or words to that effect. He explains in as calm a voice as he can manage that they can still fly the plane using brute force, but the plane has no wheel brakes and they can't lower the landing gear or dump extra fuel.

All the airports along the Pacific Coast were fogged in, so we flew around for a bit before Spokane, Washington, gave us the green light. Their runway was no great shakes, but it ended at a plowed farmer's field, so this wounded bird could skid for miles if it had to. The pilot's last message was that the co-pilot was down in the hatch, hand-cranking the landing gear, but we'd have no way of knowing if it was locked in place until we landed.

Seconds later, a black strip appears under us, and the plane drops like a 200,000-pound anvil. Flashing red lights from fire trucks and ambulances are dotted along the runway. We're still going a million miles an hour, all wobbly, but we're sitting level and there are no grinding sounds through the floor, so the landing gear must have held.

We finally came to a stop, nose down, in the farmer's field, with strips of chain link fence draped over the nose. We were all off that plane *tout suite*. Now, that trip was downright dangerous.

Then there was the time I flew into Edmonton, hours after a tornado had just ripped through. All us passengers figured that our little tin tube was going to shake itself to pieces. Now that's dangerous!

I also flew from Vancouver to Quesnel on a four-engine prop job that crossed through a violent storm front, and the plane dropped so suddenly that a newborn baby lying in a passenger's lap hit the ceiling and cigarette butts flew out of the ashtrays. Even the pilots were amazed that the wings didn't snap off. That was dangerous too.

But trucking through the old Moose and Bacon?

No sweat!

CHECK *THAT* OUT!

FOR BETTER OR WORSE, OUR DIESEL-GOBBLING big rigs sure do get lots of attention. I suppose some of the motoring public sees us as noisy, slow-moving spray manufacturers, but even those folks look us over as they struggle to pass. In my humble opinion, most people would love to get a shot at driving one of our wingless 747s.

The mere size of our present-day rigs demands attention. Of course, we of the Double Clutch Society look each other over like dogs in a park, showing proper respect whether the rig is old or new. Personally, when I see an old rebuilt classic, all chromed up and dripping with lights and metallic paint, I place my company cap over my heart and quietly weep as I silently thank the owner who spent the big bucks to do that.

Of course, what attracts the most attention from the masses is our hi-cube wagons. You've got to admit, one of those mobile warehouses painted whiter than a nurse's nylons, with marker lights every six inches and pulled by a shiny Whatever stands out like ketchup on a clean T-shirt.

On top of that, most of them are travelling billboards. They either advertise the company that owns the mother or flog the product that gets stuffed into her. For the most part, I search out the cab door or whatever, to see where the rig hails from. I'm in Vancouver, and when I see the guy is from Spud Patch, PEI, thoughts of being far from home creep in.

I do admit that the advertising on those wagons is brilliant. They criss-cross the old Moose and Hockey Puck, visible to millions. Not to be outdone, the tanker rigs we see are a class act. Usually, though, it's only the carrier's name splashed along that stainless steel tube. Those rigs are usually shining like the seat on cheap slacks, but other than water, milk or gas, it's wise not to advertise what's inside. Between you and me, it's a darn good thing most folks can't read a placard.

The guys who always catch old Donny's eye are the heavy equipment haulers. I've got to admit, the rigs aren't always shined up like the general freighters, but the sites those lowbeds get dragged through usually resemble pig pens.

The Alberta-based, haul-anything-anywhere outfit that I spent a good hunk of my life with had every conceivable machinery trailer built. Lucky for me, the heavy haul stuff I worked with was mostly brand new, arriving at the port of Vancouver from foreign countries. Of all the huge dozers, excavators and what-have-you, my guess would be that 50 per cent of it is built overseas. I tell you true, boys, when we're hooked to a streamlined, whole-buncha-wheels lowbed, with a humongous crawler filling the length of the floor and spilling over the sides, it's like a parade. Talk about an eye-catcher!

Mind you, the biggest attention-getter is usually when something goes haywire. A couple of our guys loaded up one of those big war-machine-type tanks a bunch of years back at the army base near Wainright, Alberta. Darn thing filled the floor and weighed somewhere around eighty thousand pounds. The boys were getting a little peckish and figured that the gizmo would stay put without chains, so they headed the whole thing into town to eat. A little miscalculation at a tight right turn and the trailer crawls up a high curb. Those mud-died-up old tracks had no sticktion and off she slid!

The tank was indestructible, so the only damage done was a new pothole in the pavement. Every soul in town came for a peek as it hung there—one track on the trailer and one on the street—waiting for a soldier to reload her. The only good thing about this shemozzle was that one of the company owners was driving. Had it been one of us coolies, there would have been an execution!

First prize for gawker appeal has to go to a load we hauled on one of these low-slung wagons a couple of years back. NASA in the States hired our company to haul their space shuttle "Orbiter" from Houston, Texas, to a display site in Calgary. It had to move in one piece, wings and all, which made for a pretty massive chunk. Sitting on our specially-designed rig, it measured 15 feet high, 26 feet wide and it weighed 30 tons. It took the guys a week and a half to make a trip that's usually done in three days. If you tried to haul something this size for anyone but the United States government, you'd have ended up in the slammer, but the special permit they carried left the dozen or so cops that stopped them grumbling to themselves. You can just imagine the oogling that baby got.

Last, but not least, are the flatdeck yankers. Granted, it's pretty hard to paint them up like a dry box or to stick signs all over them, but the tractors are just as classy and some of the freight demands a little attention.

For instance, did you ever see an ocean-going freighter's anchor? Brother, they're massive, and we ended up with six of these to move from Vancouver up to the Arctic for an offshore oil drilling ship. Usually this kind of stuff was loaded on a barge and floated up, but the oil company hollered "rush!" so overland they went.

These anchors look like a capital T with pointed flutes sticking out and they weigh about twenty tons each. We had to cut holes in the decks and stick one flute down within two feet of the ground to sit them solid. I'd hate to count the times we'd hear "Boys, you're going the wrong way! The ocean is that direction!" Warped truckers' humour, I guess.

Speaking of oil companies, between them and the big construction guys, they sure keep our flatdeck fleet hopping. Not only do they come up with some of the weirdest-shaped freight, they also come up with massive amounts of it. Some of the mega-projects we've hauled boggle the mind.

For example, the machinery for the Northern Alberta Tar Sands projects came from all over the world and amounted to thousands of loads. The steel work for the

Vancouver International Airport expansion was pre-fabbed in Edmonton and trucked out. Hundreds of loads! The steel work for the West Edmonton Mall expansion was pre-fabbed in Vancouver and trucked out. Hundreds of loads! The prefab concrete slabs for the Microsoft expansion in Washington State were trucked from Calgary. Again, hundreds of loads! The majority of piping for the new Shell Refinery outside Edmonton was pre-fabbed in Texas and trucked up. Hundreds of loads! Go figure why projects have to move so far, but hey—it's good for business. Flatdecks *rule*, dudes.

Speaking of weird freight, I'm going to blow some sunshine up my own dress. We trucked plate steel from the Port of Vancouver to one of the big steel outfits in Alberta. Most of it was gravy, but the eighteen-foot-wide stuff was four feet over the BC laws. The railroad propped it up on an angle in gondola cars, but slow service backed up the orders something fierce. Old Donny here messes with some drawings, figures a way to slant these monsters on a Super B and sent the plans to the steel company. Mr. Big phones me days later, tells me that a set of these racks are being built as we speak, and that my company has the contract for all the wide stuff. Gang, those racks are still running steady and Old Donny comes out looking like a genius! For heaven's sake, don't tell them the truth.

Gang, if you want to attract attention, fly down the road with a load of slanted plate. We should charge for the show.

FREIGHTLINER "U"

WE'VE GOTTA PUT A ROTTEN RUMOUR DOWN THE drain, gang. There are a few misinformed folks out there who think we drive trucks for a living because we couldn't find steady work somewhere else. Bull biscuits! Pure hogwash!

Just think about it. Who in his or her right mind would sit on forty tons of snarling steel, hurling down a road you can barely see because of yet another snow storm? We do it because we love it, buddy! Although most of us make a darn good living at this, very few get rich from it, so it sure as hell ain't the money. You just have to love it, amigo.

There are no merit badges, silver stars on our trip reports, or promotions to admiral for years behind the gears. We just love it.

I suppose none of us are born with diesel coarsing through our veins, but the ones who choose our trade are usually lifers. I'll be the first to admit that commanding one of our earth-bound battleships isn't for everyone. There are a handful of folks who go through the trouble and expense to train, get the proper license and search out a driving job, only to discover it's not their thing. It all looks pretty routine from the sidewalk, I imagine, but when something goes *gerstunken*, it usually separates the truckers from the telemarketers. Bummer! I can imagine their stories aren't pretty.

There are drivers with families who find that the time away from home becomes a problem and turn in their fuel cards, but usually they end up city driving or short hauling because they still love the work.

We've been labelled with the word "transient," which suggests that drivers come and go like memos in the lunch room. Manure muffins!

Truth is, a lot of our hi-milers have other occupations or responsibilities and are only available certain times of the year. Farmers, for instance, have to plant crops in spring and harvest in fall. The rest is left up to God and hail insurance, so they have months available to make miles. Construction guys and other seasonal types can truck all winter—or all summer if they're skidoo salesmen. They come back every year, regular as fleas on a stray kitten. Matter of fact, all kinds of these "transients" drop their first occupation and take the truckers' oath: "Thou shalt not sack others on a double solid line, nor shall ye lie about your horsepower." Farmers are famous for trading the inherited acres and Massey Ferguson for a fire-belching Freightliner and never regretting it for a second.

I certainly realize that some of the spareboarders we get would be nuts to quit Job One. Pensions and gold-plated benefits can't be ignored, right? This brings me to another huge point about our image. First, to quote the bleeding obvious, none of us are born mileage merchants. If your old man owns a couple of pebble packers (dump trucks, okay?) you may end up trucking right out of school, but the rest of us have to kill time until we reach eighteen to get our wings. Then we wait into our twenties before a company will cut us loose with an eighteen-wheeler.

Friends, you will not believe the list of occupations our pedal squeezers had before they got addicted to diesel fuel. Trucking with these guys was not just a high point of my career, but I learned more about the world than any schooling could ever cover. Matter of fact, when I turned fifteen, I was convinced that there was nothing else to learn and I quit school to do dead-end jobs until I could truck!

Bar none, every trucker I ever spoke to or teamed with had fascinating pre-trucking stories. Chrome Stack, Zorro, Little John, and a bunch of others were ex-farmers who were right at home travelling in the middle of nowhere. They could repair anything that broke, paid no attention to the Prairie cold and could sense a storm coming when there wasn't a cloud in the sky. I sure understood why they decided to hi-mile after hearing about damaged crops and hard times.

Gold-digger Pat flew a PWA 707 and J.B. flew an L1011 for Canadian Air. Both these pilots got heaps of time off and mixed gears to fill in the time. They flew all over the world and their stories of weird places and near misses still come to my mind. Fat bucks and early retirement kept them flying, but they still craved eighteen-wheeling.

Mac and a few others were ex-RCMP cops. Their behind-the-scenes police stories would hold my attention for hours. Biggest problem teaming with them was that everyone in a truck stop would look shifty and dangerous to me. Hey! I wasn't scared. I was with a Mountie!

Rick, Inky, Markie, and a bunch of others were professional hockey players. You could tell from the missing teeth, bent beaks, and stiff ankles. These guys could keep you in stitches for hours, telling about the trouble they'd get into before, during, and after their games. Old hockey players don't die, they just go trucking!

For my history lessons, I had the likes of Rick, Layosh, and Jesse, who trucked all over Europe and Africa. If you think we have it rough here in the Big C, a team trip with one of these guys will curl your drive shaft.

Hydraulic Jack and Yabadaba were both bus drivers who decided that the peace and quiet of a Kenworth was a whole lot better than a bus. Buddy, if you figure truckers do silly things, wait until these guys spill what the general public pulls off. Tsk, tsk!

You want to team drive with someone who'll keep you awake and alert for hours? Try Rocky (affectionately nicknamed "Sowbelly"), who was a Canadian army commando during the Korean War. The things this guy talks about would make a coroner cringe.

Speaking of coroners, one of the guys I enjoyed teaming

with more than any was Crazy Nicky. The guy's family ran a funeral home and ambulance service in a small Alberta town, so good old Nicky was a licensed undertaker. He had big, brown, sad eyes and looked a bit like Boris Karloff, which made his stories all the more creepy. He would speak of a dearly-departed having to be cut down from a tree, where the corpse had hung for a week in the forest. Vivid details about the sound a body makes when it hits the tarp were nothing unusual to Nicky. Preparing bodies for an open coffin funeral when they had to get inventive because there were parts missing was another interesting topic.

Nicky finally admitted to giving up undertaking because he found that some among the living were more fun! I kind of figure he told me all this stuff so I'd stay awake and keep wheeling. He could sleep like a baby in that bunk, which amazed me, considering what he had done for a living.

Compared to Nicky, I led a pretty ho-hum life. The only thing that comes close was one of my first jobs out of school. I drove a small delivery truck for a flower shop in Edmonton (I heard that snicker! How'd you like to tiptoe through this, Tiny Tim?)

Anyway, the florist's biggest customers were funeral homes, and the wreaths or whatever were usually kept in the same fridge as the person they were meant for. Took a little getting used to for a sixteen-year-old kid to struggle by the steel table when the recently-demised was being readied for the send-off.

So help me, I learned more making miles with all these

different guys than any college could have provided. Truck stories are still the best ones, and jokers like Sparky make the job fun. We never got any lawyers or politicians in our business, but we had to draw the line somewhere, eh gang?

Heck, we don't need to go to other occupations. They all come to us!

EPILOGUE

I HATE BEING THE BEARER OF BAD NEWS, BUT THIS is the last page, gang. I enjoyed every minute of having you along for the ride and really hope you got a few laughs and a peek inside the trucking business. I've enjoyed your company. I hope you'll consider climbing into the jump seat and joining me again in the future.

—Don McTavish

Rod, you were dead right! This book needs a
GLOSSARY

A-train—two trailers with tow bar axel in middle

anchor—stop the rig

axel—set of four wheels

B-train—two trailers with two axels in middle

banjo—rear end casings

bed bug—furniture hauler

binders—brakes

bobtail—travel without a trailer

bogie—group of wheels

boomer—tie-down chain tightener

bubble gum—revolving, roof-mounted light

cabover—flat-faced truck (engine under)

china top—hard-top trailer with curtain sides

conventional—long-nosed truck (engine ahead)

cup and saucer—bunk mounts on log trucks

deadhead—travel with empty trailer

deck—flatdeck with open trailer

diff lock—power transfer to extra wheel

doghouse—engine cover in cabover

dynamite—cut air to brake system

fifth wheel—device connecting truck to trailer

flip-flop—return trip

fridge—reefer (refrigerated trailer)

gag and heave—truck stop restaurant

glad hands—airline connectors to trailer

go-backwards—large, outside mirrors

graze—eat meals

Great Dane—semi-trailer brand name

headache rack—driver protection frame behind cab

hi-cube—enclosed trailer with no heating or cooling

hi-miler—long distance truck driver

jack knife—truck and trailer form capital L shape

jewellery—tire chains

K-wobbler—slang for Kenworth

log book—driver's daily record (by law)

long legs—geared for higher speeds

lowbed—low-slung, heavy equipment trailer

pebble merchant—gravel hauler

pole—trailer for log haul

pong axel—an add-on tractor axle

possum belly—drop centre van for furniture haul

rag top—canvas roof trailer (overtop loading)

sack—pass another vehicle

single drop—three-foot high trailer

skins—worn tires

slush box—torque converter (automatic transmission)

snipe—bar used to close chain boomer

sow—oversized field truck

squirrels—low-powered gas engine

stack—chrome exhaust extension

stool pigeon—tachometer (records trip details)

Super B—two-trailer set, 3-axle centre

tandem—set of eight wheels

tag-axle—airlifted, extra axle on truck

thumper—hammer to check for flat tire

tractor—truck rigged to pull semi-trailer

U-drive—belts providing power to rear add-on truck axle

westcoasters—large outside mirrors

Well known for his joke- and storytelling abilities, **Don McTavish** was employed in almost every aspect of the trucking industry from 1958 to 1997. Encouraged by friends and family to document his wacky and funny trucking experiences, McTavish originally found a place for his stories in the trucking trade magazine *Highway Star,* where he writes a feature section entitled "This Ain't No Bull." Born in Calgary, Alberta, Don is now retired and lives in Vancouver, British Columbia, with his wife Marg. He spends his time writing, puttering, and staying in touch with his friends, two adult children, and four grandchildren.